IN THE COMPANY
OF WRITERS
— 2010

IN THE COMPANY OF WRITERS

2010

MEADOW BROOK WRITING PROJECT

iUniverse, Inc.
Bloomington

In the Company of Writers 2010

iUniverse books may be ordered through booksellers or by contacting:

iUniverse
1663 Liberty Drive
Bloomington, IN 47403
www.iuniverse.com
1-800-Authors (1-800-288-4677)

Because of the dynamic nature of the Internet, any Web addresses or links contained in this book may have changed since publication and may no longer be valid. The views expressed in this work are solely those of the author and do not necessarily reflect the views of the publisher, and the publisher hereby disclaims any responsibility for them.

Any people depicted in stock imagery provided by Thinkstock are models, and such images are being used for illustrative purposes only.

Certain stock imagery © Thinkstock.

ISBN: 978-1-4759-3840-1 (sc)
ISBN: 978-1-4759-3841-8 (e)

Printed in the United States of America

iUniverse rev. date: 7/10/2012

Credit for graphics: Dover Electronic Clip Art, Dover Publications, Inc.

Beginnings

Everything starts from something,

no matter how big or small

Everything starts from something,

from a book to a worm to a wall.

What can you start from something?

Imagine anything at all…

By Dawn Dobija

Acknowledgments

The summer of 2010 would not have been the same without Meadow Brook Writing Project's co-directors, Mary Cox and Kathleen Reddy-Butkovich. They have a gift for creating an environment that encourages productive, passionate discussion and writing. Not only did we learn much and write a lot, but we all grew as individual teachers and writers in our close-knit, eclectic group. We couldn't have had as much fun with professional development as we did with these two amazing women.

We also wish to thank Marshall Kitchens, the director of the Meadow Brook Writing Project. We are lucky to have a director who truly values our ideas and opinions. He cares about our writing community, and is very willing to support our endeavors in building a stronger cohort of writers and writing teachers.

Most importantly, we need to thank the teachers, students, parents, friends, family, writers, administration, and everyone else who value writing. Writing is not only a cornerstone in our education, but in the way we connect as human beings. Without this realization, we would have no audience for our book.

We will never lose our passion for writing. Thank you, writers, readers, and teachers.

CONTENTS

Preface

"Before I start, I want to explain…"
Ours was the summer of the preface.

After pouring time and ourselves into a piece of writing, momentarily brushing aside the flakes of insecurity and self-doubt floating around our heads, we had to sit in front of a group of people we barely knew and read it. Aloud. When it came time to open ourselves and share what we wrote, the unassuredness settled heavily, wrapping its arms around our necks to secure its place.

And so we prefaced. We made sure our audience knew we weren't fooling ourselves into thinking we had written a masterpiece. It was our way of saying, "It's okay if you think my writing is horrible, I maybe, possibly, do I?, think so, too." We were bracing ourselves for rejection. For many of us, our writing was personal, sharing things about ourselves we rarely did elsewhere, whether directly through narrative, or more subtly through voice and theme. Writing opens doors to parts of ourselves we sometimes neglect or have a difficult time communicating. We were often accessing our vulnerabilities, and then deepening that by displaying them, naked, to people we'd only just met.

And yet, following these prefaces in which we opened ourselves up more, perhaps, than our stories and poetry themselves, we read. They were masterpieces, not by the standards of publishers and bestseller lists, but for us, the eclectic group of Writing and Writer Teachers of the MBWP 2010 Summer Institute. Author's Chair awakened something in us, something butterfly-ISH emerging from our pages and mouths. Not only did we revive our writer selves, but something more, something deeper.

It sounds cliched to say we laughed and cried together. Those words don't quite evoke the feelings and paint the scene the way only *being there* can. But we did laugh and cry, every week, often within minutes, moved and entertained by the writings of each other, and by the bonds that were forming.

By the end of the month our prefaces were less insecurity and more trust, an explanation in the way of talking to someone you know well, someone who just *gets* it. So the preface of this book is not an excuse. It is not a warning that what you are about to read might not be that good. This preface, followed by a glorious collection of our writing, is an exultation. Like peering through the windows of Frances Dodge's playhouse, consider yourself honored to catch a glimpse into our summer, our group, our writing.

Thank you for reading,
Christina Hall

CHAPTER 1

DAWN DOBIJA

What Makes a Writer

Do diplomas make a writer,
or Le Cordon Bleu make a chef?
Does med school make a doctor,
or ref school make a ref?
Do universities make a teacher,
walking through hallowed halls?
What really makes us what we are,
what really makes us stall?
Does writing make a writer,
or cooking make a chef?
Does practicing medicine make a doctor,
or reffing make a ref?
Does teaching make a teacher,
who starts over every fall?
Does trying make us better,
and should we try it all?

Learning

An idea is a smoldering ember,
each thought a popping spark.
As learning starts the fire grows bolder,
calling us in from the dark.
To feed this fire we need knowledge,
we need to teach to make our mark.
Education is never ending,
like the song of a noble lark.

If I were Spiderman

"Look out!" I yelled as I raced zigzagging down the hallway. I move fastest when I am Spiderman like I am right now, using my shiny strong webs to swing from. No one can catch me.

"I'm here," I yelled as I zoomed into my classroom door.

"Good morning, Jeremiah," called out Miss Kate. She's my teacher.

"I'm not Jeremiah; I'm Spiderman today."

"Okay, Spiderman," Miss Kate said with a smile.

"Where is your mom?"

"Probably still at the car. She's so slow, she can't keep up with me."

"Jeremiah," Miss Kate said with a disapproving look on her face. "We've talked about this before. What are you supposed to do when you get out of your car?"

"Stay with Mama until I get all the way to the classroom. I know," I mumbled, "and I told you I am Spiderman today not Jeremiah!"

"I just want you to make it to class safely, Spiderman, not squished by a car or snatched up by a bad guy. I would be so sad if anything happened to you. I really like when you are here in class with me."

"Okay," I said smiling sheepishly, "I promise."

Just then Mama walked in the classroom talking on her phone like always. Miss Kate said "Good Morning, Miss Williams. Can I talk to you for a quick minute please?"

Mama looked up with her annoyed face and said, "Can't. In a hurry," and continued to talk on her phone.

"Okay, but please make sure to stay with Jeremiah all the way to the classroom, maybe hold his hand," said Miss Kate following Mama to the door. "We've had some incidents in the parking lot, and I want to make sure he's safe."

Mama waved her hand, not even looking, to let Miss Kate know she heard her. I wandered over to get my set up for breakfast bowl, spoon and napkin. I sat down at the table next to Shaniece. I like her, but sometimes she's mean to me and tells me I'm not her friend. I wonder if I'm her friend today.

"What's for breakfast?"

"It's Monday, what do we always have for breakfast on Mondays," asked Miss Kate?

"Cereal," I replied making a yucky face. "I hate cereal."

"Well, you might like this kind; it's the kind that talks to you," she said making her eyes all big.

"Really?" I asked. "What's it say?"

"I don't know. You'll have to listen really carefully when you poor in the milk."

I scooped cereal into my bowl and poured the milk. Sure enough, the cereal starting snapping and crackling. Whoa, this is so cool. I moved my ear right up to the bowl to listen.

"My cereal is saying something, Miss Kate. You want to know what it's saying?" I asked.

"Miss Kate is talking to D'Onte's Mama," Shaniece said. "She's not listening to you."

"So," I said. "She'll want to know when she's done."

Shaniece moved her bowl and turned so her back was to me and started talking to someone else.

"Where's Miss Jenny?" I asked. Maybe she would want to hear what my cereal was telling me.

"She went to the office, she'll be right back," Jack told me from the Lego table.

Shaniece stood up and said, "Miss Kate, did you know I'm four now?"

"That's right, you had a birthday over the weekend. We'll have to sing to you at circle time," she said.

"So what, I'm four, too. Big deal. Miss Kate, do you want to know what my cereal said to me?"

"In a minute, Jeremiah. I have to get more milk out. You are all as thirsty as camels today."

Why doesn't anyone want to hear about my cereal? I look over at Shaniece who is telling whoever will listen that she got a princess dress for her birthday. I bet if she made some noise then someone would pay attention. I stood up and shoved Shaniece hard, and she fell out of her chair with a scream just as Miss Jenny walked back in the room. I sat in my chair quickly as Miss Jenny yelled, "Jeremiah, what'd you do that for? You know better than that. Come over here and tell Shaniece you're sorry for pushing her."

But I'm not sorry, I thought. I got up anyway. "Sorry, Shaniece," I muttered so quietly that is was barely above a whisper.

"I'm all right," she snapped, "but don't you push me again!"

Then I looked up at Miss Jenny and said, "You wanna know what my cereal said to me?"

She looked at me and smiled with her head shaking back and forth and said, "Sure, tell me what your cereal said."

"It told me that I can go faster than Spiderman," I whispered excitedly.

"I bet you can. Now go clean up your place, and let's go build with Legos until circle time starts.

Circle time and work time flew by. I got to pick a song to sing at circle time, and I picked the Johnny pounds song. Everyone looks so funny when they are pounding hammers with their hands, feet and head. It makes me laugh every time. Then at work time Shaniece told me I had to be her boyfriend and buy her presents, so Jack helped me build a fort to hide from her. I was invisible when I was in my fort, and she couldn't make me do anything. We had clean up time which I hate, but I always clean up fast because after that we always go outside. I love going outside. I can climb to the top of the structure faster than anyone, just like Spiderman.

"I'm going to be Spiderman when we get outside," I told Jack.

"Cool, I wanna be Spiderman too."

"You can't; you're too slow. You can be batman instead."

"Okay," he said glumly, "but tomorrow can I be Spiderman?"

"Maybe," I told him. "We'll see."

I was at the top of the climber whispering to Jack about who the next bad guy was going to be when D'Onte came over and said, "Me play?"

"No, you're just a baby," I told him. "Go play with the other babies."

"No, me play Spiderman!" he demanded stubbornly.

"Leave us alone," I yelled at him, but he wouldn't stop following us. So I turned around and pushed him. He stumbled and fell and started crying so loud. *Great,* I thought, *now we'll really be in trouble.*

"Run, Jack," I yelled and flew down the slide trying to get as far away from D'Onte as possible. I guess I didn't get far enough because Miss Kate caught up to me, and she was really mad.

"Jeremiah, that is the second time today that you pushed someone. I am so disappointed. What is going on with you today?" she asked.

"Nothing," I told her as I was looking at the ground kicking a pebble.

"Well, I think we are going to have to talk to your mom about your behavior at school. You can't keep hurting your classmates. They need to feel safe when they are at school, too, just like you should."

"NOOO," I wailed. "You can't tell Mama; I'll be good. I promise. Please don't tell her," I cried. I couldn't stop crying. Tears poured down my face, dropping off of my chin. "Please," I whispered, pleading.

I didn't want to go inside. Once we get in there, we eat lunch, and then it's time to go. I didn't want to go home. When Mama finds out I was cutting up in school, she is going to whoop me so hard. She says when I'm bad I make her look like a bad mama, and she already has enough to deal with. I tried hiding under the climber, but Miss Jenny dragged me out. At least she is letting me hold her hand and walk as slow as I want back to our room. I don't want to eat. I just pick at my food while everyone around me is eating and talking. No one even notices me. I ask Miss Kate if I can be done and go look at a book. Maybe if I'm way over in the corner Mama won't see me, and I can just stay here all night. She nods yes, and I hurry over to the corner where I bury myself under the bean bags and try not to move.

I don't hear Mama come in, and it isn't until Miss Jenny says, "Here he is playing hide and seek," that I climb out all sweaty and hot from the bean bags. I could see from the look on Mama's face that they already told her what happened.

"Boy!" she said. "You'd best apologize to your teachers for how you acted today."

"I'm sorry," I said quietly. "I promise it won't happen again."

I looked up at Mama to see if I had said enough. She nodded once, and Miss Kate said, "Thank you, Jeremiah. Tomorrow is a new day, and I am looking forward to having fun with you."

"See you tomorrow," Miss Kate and Miss Jenny said at the same time.

Mama put her hand on the back of my neck and pushed me out of the door.

"What'd I tell you about makin' me look bad, boy? You know you're gonna get whooped tonight, don't ya?"

She was squeezing my neck hard as we walked to the car.

I know, Mama, I'm sorry."

"Not as sorry as you're gonna be," she said. "Now no more cuttin' up while you're at Granny's this afternoon. She's too old to deal with that. And uncle JJ won't be home from school til three."

"What? I have to go to Granny's?"

I hate going there. She is so old she can hardly move, and it is so boring. She naps in her chair the whole time, and if I try to turn the channel from her stories, she wakes up and yells at me. Plus, she smells like she peed on herself.

When we get to Granny's, Mama doesn't even get out of the car. She just pulls in the driveway, tells me to get out, and leaves. I go to the door and open it.

"Granny, are you here?" I yell as I walk in.

"Huh, what's that? Oh, it's you Jeremiah. What are you doin' here, and where's your mama?"

"Mama just dropped me off and left," I told her.

"Coletta that good for nothing little tramp," Granny mumbled under her breath shaking her head.

"What?" I asked.

"Nothing. Come in. How was school today?"

"Fine," I told her. "Can I watch cartoons?"

"For a few minutes. My stories are comin' on."

I settled on the couch and turned on the TV. I couldn't find anything on but baby shows, so when Granny came back in a few minutes later I gave her the remote. I sat for a few minutes watching her show, but it's just people kissing and touching each other in bed, or people yelling and fighting about nothing. I closed my eyes and started thinking about what it would be like to really be Spiderman.

I woke up to the sound of someone coming in the door. "Uncle JJ!" I cried.

"Hey, Little Man, what you doin' here, your mama out skankin' again?"

"Huh?" I asked.

"Never mind. You wanna come hang with me til your mama gets here?"

"Really, can I?"

"Sure, come on. I'll show you somethin' new I got."

JJ stands for Jeremiah James. I'm named after him, and he is 16 and the coolest guy I've ever met. We went down to the basement where uncle JJ's bedroom is. It is the coolest place. He has posters and cool clothes and a great stereo. He puts on some music, but not too loud so he doesn't wake up Granny.

"Okay, Little Man, if I show you this you gotta promise not to tell anyone ever, got it?"

"I promise, Uncle JJ, I am really good at keepin' secrets."

"Okay," he says as he picks up his back pack and puts it on the bed.

As he unzips it, I can feel my stomach start to flutter with anticipation. I wonder if he has something magic in there. When he starts to pull it out I see that it's black, and then my eyes almost pop out. It's a gun!

"Uncle JJ, what you doin' with a gun? Guns are bad. I learned in school from Eddie Eagle that I should tell if I see a gun," I exclaim fearfully.

"Come on, Little Man. I thought you were gonna be cool. I thought you were old enough for me to show this to."

"I am," I said quickly. I wanted to be cool, but I was really scared. I know that guns can hurt people really bad.

"Do you want to touch it?" he asked.

"Okay," I said, wanting to make uncle JJ proud of me for being brave. I put out one finger and moved it slowly toward the gun. Right when I touched it, Uncle JJ yelled, "Bang!" He laughed as I started crying.

"I'm just messin' with ya, Little Man. You're safe. You're always safe with Uncle JJ. You tell me if anyone messes with you, and I'll take care of them. All right?"

I sniffed and nodded yes and then heard my mama yell from upstairs. "Gotta go," I said racing up the stairs.

"Catch ya later Little Man," Uncle JJ yelled behind me.

Mama and I got in the car. "We goin' home now?" I asked hopefully.

"Yep, now hush up. I got a call to make."

Mama is always on the phone. I usually don't even listen, but today she was talking about me.

"I swear I'm always havin' to deal with some shit. The boy was cuttin' up in school again today. I wish I could get rid of him like I did his sister. \I got her daddy to take her off my hands, but his daddy's in jail again, so I'm stuck. It'd be a lot easier to get things done, I tell ya."

I stopped listening then, thinking she didn't really want to get rid of me. Did she? I try to be good. I really do. I guess I better try really, really hard. I don't want to go live anywhere else. I don't want to go away from Mama. I can feel the tears start, but I can't let her see them, so I dash them away quick and try to think about Spiderman.

When we get home, I ask Mama what we're eating for supper. "I've got friends comin' over. Anything you find in there you can eat, and then you put yourself in your room and don't come out for nothing, you hear me?"

"Not even to pee?" I asked.

She rolls her eyes at me and says, "Yes, you can come out to pee. You damn well better not pee on yourself."

I remind myself I am being really good and just head into the kitchen to look for food. There is nothing in the refrigerator but ketchup, hot sauce and cheese. I pull out the cheese. There is bread in the cupboard, but it's moldy. I guess I can pull off the moldy parts. I get a plate, three pieces of bread and two pieces of cheese. I am so hungry. I haven't eaten anything since breakfast.

I go to my room and shut the door, just like Mama told me. I have my own bed; it's just a mattress on the floor, but it's just mine, and I have two blankets. One is a Spiderman blanket. It's my favorite. I also have a TV that you can put tapes in. Mama says it's so I can watch my movies and not bother her. I am going to be so quiet tonight she won't even know I'm here. I also have all my guys. I have three Spiderman guys and lots of others. I put in the Spiderman movie and eat my dinner. Mama comes in and says, "My friends are gonna be here in a minute. Do not come out for anything but the bathroom. Even if you hear yellin' or loud noises, you stay in your room no matter what, okay?"

"Yes Mama," I said. She left and shut the door.

A little while later, I can hear the music from the other room. It is so loud it makes the whole house shake. I hear people, too, laughing and talking really loud. I get right in front of my TV. With the volume all the way up, I can barely hear it. I watch one Spiderman movie and then another. Mama's friends are still here. I can feel the loud music in my chest. I lie on my bed and try to think about being Spiderman for real. Everyone would love me if I was Spiderman. Soon I start to doze off. A little while later I am woken up by the sound of glass breaking and someone screaming. It sounds like Mama. There are more sounds I don't recognize, dull thuds and grunts and more stuff breaking. People are yelling. I hear a man's voice. I can't hear what they are saying over the music. More screaming. I am so scared. I want to make sure Mama is okay, but I have to be good. I have to stay here like I promised I would. I don't want her to get rid of me.

After some time, the sound of things breaking and the screaming stops. All I hear is the music. I don't know what to do. I am scared for Mama. I think there was a monster in the house, and I think Mama could be hurt. But I promised I'd stay in my room, so I take my Spiderman blanket and cram myself between the mattress and the wall in case the monster comes in here too. He won't be able to see me over here under the blanket. I am so quiet so no one would ever hear me. I hope the monster is gone. I hold my breath until I can't any longer and just hope that Mama is okay. I stay like this until the sun starts to peek through my window. It's tomorrow. I think I should go out there. I think I need to see if Mama is okay. I need her to take me to school. I have to show everyone that I am a good boy so I can stay with Mama.

I slowly open my door, and the music is still on. I creep quietly down the hall to the living room. I go to the stereo and turn it off; now it is silent. I am shaking, and I turn around slowly and see Mama lying on the couch. Her face is purple and blue, and blood is dried on her lips. Her clothes are ripped. The table is covered with bottles that have some yucky smelling stuff in them. Lots of them are broken, and brown stuff drips down the wall. Two of the chairs are broken into pieces. I go to Mama and poke her gently. "Mama," I whisper, "Mama, are you okay?" She grunts and I start to cry. I don't know what to do.

"Mama, are you going to take me to school today?"

She just grunts at me again. I think about what I can do to show her I'm a good boy. I start picking up all the broken glass and putting it in the trash. Then I get my Spiderman blanket and put it over Mama in case she is cold. I work for a long time and get most of the mess cleaned up, at least the parts I can reach and lift. I think about calling Uncle JJ but don't know how to use Mama's phone. I bring Mama some water and try to wake her up again. This time she opens her eyes, looks at me, takes the water, and starts to cry.

"Thanks, Baby," she says with her voice cracking, and I am able to breathe for the first time all day.

After this, Mama gets up and cleans up the rest and goes to bed in her room. I eat the rest of the moldy bread and cheese and go to bed, too. I don't think it's bed time yet, but I am so tired I don't even care. I close my eyes and all I can see are monsters. I open them up again and think I am never going to close them again. I put on one of my movies and wish hard to become Spiderman so that I can save my mama from the monsters. I watch it over and over until I see the sun shine in the window again.

Today I am very quiet. I get dressed and brush my teeth and hair all by myself. Then I go to see if Mama is up.

"Mama, are you up?" I ask. "Am I going to go to school today?"

"Huh, oh give me a minute and I'll take you."

I close her door and go wait for her on the couch. I hear her go in the bathroom and back to her room. I am afraid she forgot me when she finally comes out.

"Get in the car. Let's go," she says.

I say nothing and run to the car. I hope she can see what a good boy I've been. She gets on the phone on the way to school.

At least things are getting back to normal. When we get to school, I remember what Miss Kate told me, and I walk over to Mama and take her hand. She looks down at me and runs her hand over my head and then puts her hand in mine. Nothing has ever felt better. We walk to my class holding hands, and on the way Mama says, "You've been a big boy lately. Now you know it's nobody's business what happens at home, right? Anyone asks, you just tell them your mama was sick yesterday, got it?"

"Yes, Mama," I said, and we walked in.

Miss Kate greeted me with a big hug and a smile.

"Hi, Jeremiah. I'm so glad you're back. Were you sick?"

I looked at Mama as she is walking out and yell, "Bye, Mama." She smiled and waved, and I turned back to Miss Kate and said, "No, but Mama was, and I took care of her, just like Spiderman would."

"Yes, I noticed that your mama had some boo-boos on her face. You know that you can talk to Miss Jenny and me about anything, anything at all."

"I know," I said. "But right now I'm starving. What's for breakfast?" I asked Miss Kate.

"Pancakes, your favorite," and she put three of them on my plate. "I am so happy you are back at school," said Miss Kate.

I am, too, I thought, and smiled my best good boy smile at her, just like Spiderman would.

The Day She Was Born

Nine years ago in July of 1969, my beautiful wife Cathy and I gave birth to our second son. Two boys fifteen months apart, what were we thinking, right? Somehow we survived, and here, nine years later, we find ourselves with two days left, anticipating the arrival of our third child. Nine years is a really long time to wait for this I know, but this one truly is a miracle. With both my wife and I, our growing age seemed to be a factor this time, and it took a few extra years with a few more doctors and some interesting medication to perform this miracle. I am 35 years old and feeling every minute of it. I am sure that has nothing to do with all of the long nights of beers and bullshitting I have had in my life. I hope Cathy knows that it isn't likely to stop anytime soon either.

Two days left and I am walking on pins and needles. Ever been around a woman who is close to delivery? They are a scary creature, that's for sure. You never know what you are going to walk into when you come in the door. Some days she's crying, some screaming, some laughing and my favorite days, when she is feeling amorous. Although, let me tell you it gets a little awkward to get your groove on in the ninth month. Good thing for us, I am a sensitive and thoughtful husband.

Today was a tough one. She had reminded me that I was going to be in the delivery room for the whole kit n caboodle whether I liked it, or not. I put my foot down and said no way. I wasn't allowed to be in there for the first two births which was just fine with me, and I wasn't going to change it up now. Boy, did she yell. I think the neighbors on the next block heard her. What, is she crazy? How could I ever look at her again without thinking about what I saw? I shudder at the thought. So now I find myself across the street drinking beers with Buck and Jim. They aren't much help either. They think I should do it. Watch the birth of this baby. Jim is even offering to come in with me. Amazing how brave a few beers make a man. He doesn't have kids yet.

I finished my beer and went home to bed. Poor Cathy was up half the night. I swear she goes to the bathroom every five minutes. At 6:15am she woke me up. "I'm having contractions," she said. "Get up and help me time them. " With a yawn and a scratch, I sat up and got my watch. "Okay," I said, "Tell me when to start."

Three hours later they were still too far apart to do anything about.

So, Cathy called her Doctor and asked him what to do. He suggested that we go for a walk, that it can sometimes help things progress. So off we go. Cathy wants to walk the grounds at Cranbrook, saying at least she can look at pretty things when she is doubled over in pain. We started walking at 10:00am. It was so slow and kind of chilly. Nothing happened for six long hours and then finally in a disgusting whoosh of fluid, her water broke. Thank God, that seemed to take forever. Then I remembered and muttered, "Oh shit." Cathy looked at me a little wildly as the realization that the car was parked about two miles away hit us both. "I'll be back as soon as I can," I yelled as I took off in a sprint. I think I ran those two miles faster than anyone has ever run. It seemed like ten miles by the time I made it to the car. I made it back to Cathy and off we were to the hospital.

So, the decision was made with no argument once we arrived in the hospital. I was ushered into the room right behind Cathy by the nurses. No one would pay any attention to my protests. I think there was a conspiracy against me. They got Cathy changed and prepped for the doctor in an efficient whirlwind. When the doctor came in for the exam, I cowered in the corner. What is he doing, I thought, does he really need to put his hands up there? Oh man, this is going to be a long night. I feel nauseous.

What people don't tell you about waiting to be ready to deliver is that it is the most boring, aggravating, confusing period of time ever. We went from sitting quietly so she could rest, to dealing with major contractions where she yelled and threw things, to me somehow becoming the devil incarnate. So I decided it was my job to make everyone smile. I told some of my best jokes, but they just got eye rolls. I serenaded her with my beautiful baritone voice, but I was told my songs were stupid. Then while she was napping I got my best idea. I took the box of rubber gloves over to my chair in the corner and started blowing. By the time anyone paid attention, I must have had sixteen glove balloons around me. After being reprimanded by the nurse for wasting her supplies, I sent those balloons flying all over the room, hitting them in the air, at the window, at Cathy. She looked at me strangely and all of a sudden started to giggle, then laugh, and finally downright guffaw. She was swatting at the balloons, too, and we both turned into children for a few minutes. Well, that seemed to be what pushed us around the corner because it wasn't long after that she was ready to push.

Oh crap, I am not ready for this part. I think I am going to be sick. I am standing at her shoulder, and she has two nurses holding both of her legs while the doctor sits in between them. She is sweating and screaming and grunting. I know people say this is beautiful, but it is really pretty brutal. I don't know where to look. Finally the doctor announces that the head can be seen. I suck in a breath and take a peek. Oh gross, oh God, it is like a horrible accident, I can't turn my eyes away. Here come the shoulders, we're almost there. Finally here it comes, I look and, "NO BALLS, NO BALLS," I yell, "We have a little girl!" I turn to look at Cathy, and I think we are both crying. I can't breathe and she looks relieved. "We have a little girl," I whisper. "Our little princess." She adds, "The boys are going to be so disappointed."

She was officially born at 1:01am on October 29th. I am so happy that Cathy made me stay to be a part of her birth. Just as they were moving Cathy from the delivery room back to her other room we came upon a surprise in the hallway. Standing there all suited up in scrubs and shaking like a leaf was my good buddy and neighbor Jim. "I saw your car was gone tonight and figured you must be here," he said. "How did you get into the delivery area?" I asked. "I told them I was the father, but once they were about to rush me in, I chickened out, told the truth, and have been waiting here since." I started laughing and shaking my head. "I did bring something to celebrate with though, " Jim said as he pulled a six pack of beers out from under his scrubs. "Congrats, Pat and Cathy, on your new little girl! I saw them wheel her out." He handed us each a beer. Cathy looked over at the nurse, who said, "Oh go ahead, you deserve it, and it will help with milk production. " So we clinked bottles, I let out a whoop and drank that beer. Nothing has ever tasted so refreshing.

Later, after all the calls were made and we were alone again, marveling over our new little miracle, I was hit with the enormity of this event. I have a daughter, a daughter who will wear dresses and bows and play with dolls and will someday, God forbid, want to go out with boys. This is so different then sons. I need to protect her and teach her to be strong and smart and to stand up for herself. There is so much more to think about. I kissed our girl and kissed Cathy and wandered over to the window. "Look Cathy, the sun is coming up. Isn't it beautiful?" I asked. "More beautiful than ever before," she said. "I know we agreed on Laura for a name," I said, but what do you think about Dawn?" I asked. Cathy stared out of the window at the sunrise with the sweetest look on her face and said, "You know, I think that Dawn suits her much better. Yes, our beautiful Dawn." I looked down at our little girl sleeping sweetly and was over whelmed with emotion. Later that morning while the girls slept I wrote a poem on a paper towel:

You started as a twinkle
A spark of love between us
But when you came to be
You were a sparkle
Bright and shiny
Like a thousand pink stars all clustered together
You dazzle us all
And will continue to
Forever
And thankfully we will never be the same again.

Hard Work

Searching and sneaking,
I hear my brain creaking.
Spying and trying,
I hear my brain frying.
Exuberantly seeking,
I think my brains leaking.
Exhausted and lying,
I think my brain's dying.
All work and no fun,
I think my brain's done.

CHAPTER 2

MARY COX

Lessons Learned

The day is perfect for twelve year old boys, blue sky, a touch of coolness in the air signaling the approach of fall, a bugless breeze by the stream. Two good friends fill a bucket with frogs; laughter is shared as the amphibians slip and slither between their fingers. Tennis shoes squelching, pants rolled up, jackets thrown on the bank of the stream, mud-streaked faces and t-shirts. That edge of time between boyhood and manhood when lessons learned are learned forever.

These boys, the smaller with freckles that spread across his nose and cheeks, and the taller, a towhead, have been friends since second grade when both arrived as new students in their elementary school. Star Wars action figures, Boy Scout campouts, computer games, science experiments (including damage to a mother's kitchen) have been shared for six years. They talk about being roommates in college although that time seems so far away that it hangs in the realm of fiction. Girls are still only a vague commodity to be avoided.

The three high school boys, sporting their newest tattoos, black t-shirts with cigarettes rolled into the sleeves, and the bored expressions of disenchanted youth, are drawn to the innocent laughter. The leader, a skull and cross bone earring dangling to his shoulder and a new multicolored snake tattoo on his wrist, surveys the scene with squinted eyes. The boys in the water stop. The towhead looks away, but the freckle faced boy stares eye-to-eye with snake tattoo, giving the bigger boy a reason to attack. His snake decorated arm reaches down for a rock and hurls it at the boys. The towhead jumps aside to avoid the missile. The rock hits the stream, sending a small water spout into the freckled face of the smaller boy. He steadies himself on the stream bottom, straightening his shoulders and pursing his lips. He refuses to wipe his face.

The tattooed boy steps forward, his muddy boots treading on one of the jackets. There is the unmistakable sound of breaking plastic. This sound causes the boy to pale beneath his freckles; his friend looks at him with both fear and sympathy. The snake tattoo laughs and grinds his heel in deeper, destroying the loved toy in the pocket.

Another tattooed boy, wearing a sign of a Mercedes Benz on the back of his hand, reaches for the pail of frogs. The freckled boy moves for the first time. A strangled sound comes from him as he tries to leap for the pail. He is too late. The frogs are emptied on the ground. Still dazed from being taken from their homes, they do not move. This gives the tattooed trio time to crush them. Their amphibian bodies make an unsettling, popping sound as the steel toed boots stomp and grind, stomp and grind. The freckled boy waves his arms and yells. Whether he is yelling at the boys to stop or the frogs to escape is unclear.

The freckled boy reaches the edge of the stream. The snake tattoo grabs the back of his shirt and throws him down on the muddy bank. The other boys hold the towheaded boy. With his foot in the middle of the boy's back, he tells the boy to say he is sorry he killed the frogs. The other boys laugh. The smaller boy stays quiet. They tell the towheaded friend he should tell his friend to say he is sorry. The friend does so. The smaller boy stays quiet. His quiet irritates the bigger boy and he presses his boot more deeply into his back. He tells the boy again to say he is sorry. The smaller boy stays quiet.

The first kick comes without warning. The boot catches the boy on the hip as the bigger boy yells in a rage for the boy to admit killing the frogs. Then the kicks come from all sides; the boy curls into himself for protection. He hears a bone break and realizes it is his. He tastes blood in his mouth and feels the entrails of the frog bodies on his face and soaking into his shirt as he tries to protect himself. The last thing he sees is the colorful snake wound around the shoulder of the towheaded boy as they walk away.

Chapter 3

BEN BENNETT-CARPENTER

You've Got A Picture There

You've got a picture there
on the box.

Please don't try to say there's a rationale
for every piece.

I might gobble one up
just for the act of it.
Just one lost, and what
are the other 999 to do?

But in the end we have
the same picture again,
pieced back together.
It's a closed universe
— a disappointment
moments after completion

rather than an expanding
& contracting
nether-nether-world

with Davy Crocketts
and sneakers.

I'm From The Land Of Layered Lasagna

I'm from the land of layered lasagna,
baked,
cut out
in squares, large,
measured out for each of four,
then five, then six,
from 4149 Beach Ridge Road,
North Tonawanda, New York, to
714 Hogenmiller Circle, Las Vegas,
Nevada, at the roundabout
along the fence facing
The Desert
where Donald & I
on bikes
just about lost him
when the floods rushed
through Base Housing
past the 7-11 there –
the fence no longer able
to contain
the children from the rush.

I'm from among the bubbles,
mercantile exchanges
ringing round and round –
from Hallelujah to the Cowboy
thumbing his way up The Strip.

The Table Is Laid Out

The table is laid out,
people packed in all around.
He's talked to the bride's
mother as if it's not the
first time, nor the last.
What's this familiarity
that crosses both sides
from mother's to father's
to others you've met
along the way?
Even I have a mother
and a father. I was
born, as you were,
in a backwards
place and came to
star in a minor
role as the rat.

Leave It Up

Leave it up
to the colder
places

icebergs and all

where the slide
has frozen for the time
being

and the needle points lower
than things now really stand.
The Bug, the Frog, and friends
are set there in ice for now,
set to reactivate
at first thaw.

A Cushy Timetable

A cushy timetable
rolling over, down,

100% cotton label
for the thousand percent,

the thousand thousand,
the thousand thousand
thousand
million,
for starters,

chock-full, a continent
for a mattress—

so seams mark out
the roll back and over

while the weather
just wears.

And might as well,
for what else have you to do

but parse
the beautiful onslaught
& rub toes?

CHAPTER 4

CHRISTINA HALL

Another Day

During that creation part of morning,
pinks, yellows and colors spill into the sky,
still blending themselves to cover the earth in an awakened blue sky,
and a cool mist freckles the grass and porch railings.
The air is cool,
not hesitant about clinging to your skin like a tangible promise of fresh renewal.
Barefoot wet prints in the grass offer a surreal sense of walking into a dream,
first.
The only person to glimpse this start,
a peaceful preface to choice,
moving away from stillness and just being.

And the day moves away from you, revolving while you stand, as you watch it expanding and rushing, spanning telescopic, leaving you dizzy, wanting the blank canvas lightness of morning.

Dusk approaches.
The day eases.
The sky releases a wild color frenzy to a deep dark.

Black night, absent of all color, opens up.
Silence settles, closing, slowing, exhaling.
A relieved sigh.

Gray, Ariel

Ariel tucked her hair behind her ear, and then dipped her head forward so that the brown strands brushed her cheeks once more. The basic gesture comforted her, made life seem more simple, controlled. Her colorful, quilted purse was slung over her right shoulder, her hand grasping its strap as if a mugger was going to fly by at any moment. The casual slap of her flip flops on the tiled floor made her blush. She glanced around the halls and prayed fervently she wouldn't have to come again.

She thought back to some of the last times she had been in a hospital. When her niece was born. When her grandmother was dying of cancer. How different a place could look, depending on the circumstances. She bit her tongue, inhaling slowly, attempting to release her anxiety through a long, deep, shuttering breath.

Why did she come alone?

Stop it. Stop. Have faith.

The moment she sat down, a horrible cramping gripped her stomach. She closed her eyes and tried to breathe through it. Her fingers fiddled with her purse strap. Her toes wiggled and twitched rapidly in her flip flops. She bit the inside of her lip and closed her eyes. Dammit. She wanted to cry, but instead she smiled and rose.

"Excuse me."

She walked quickly to the women's restroom and slowly closed the door.

The door closed with a gentle click. Her heart was beating louder. Ariel couldn't believe how badly her hands were shaking. She felt little, so little and unprotected. Alone.

"Gray, Ariel?" The nurse called cheerfully, as if Ariel Gray's future wasn't waiting on the other side of those doors.

By the time Ariel entered Dr. White's office, she was somewhat calmer. Whatever will be, will be, she thought foolishly.

"Have a seat."

She looked serious, and with dread, Ariel sat. She was digging her fingernails into the back of her hand when Dr. White sat on the edge of her desk.

"Ms. Gray."

"Dr. White, please…"

"Positive, Ariel. The test was positive. I'm sorry."

Positive. Ariel felt sick, not because of what the test meant, but because of what the test said. What it said about her. Her life. She opened the door and sat on the bed. Her eyes were huge and wet. At that moment, when he looked down at her, she knew he knew, and her heart fell.

Her jaw dropped and everything in her body shattered. She stared, angry, devastated. She felt her throat close immediately, and she gasped as hot tears filled her eyes. She got out of her chair quickly and turned but was only able to take a few steps before she fell to her knees, bent over in horrifying pain. The thin rug pressed through her summery skirt like sandpaper.

Her entire body convulsed. Never had she felt such pain. She screamed silently, and a deep groan emanated from her soul. Her throat burned, and a bitter taste filled her mouth. Ariel gagged as tears singed her heart.

She now felt nothing but death.

That's murder, she thought, but only nodded.

"We can't afford to have a baby, Ariel. We can barely afford this apartment. I really don't want to get married right now. Come on. I'll look it up for you. I think you can just take a pill. It'll be easy." He said it with deliberate calmness, but Ariel saw the anger behind his words. The selfish fear. He sat across from her, his elbows on his knees, pleading with her.

"Sometimes, sometimes the test is wrong. Give me a few days. Then we wouldn't even have to spend the money on an abortion." She was sobbing, pleading as well. Of course she didn't need the baby, but could she have an abortion?

Ariel knew that she would choose death. The alternative was unbearable. She left the doctor's office as soon as she stopped shaking and drove home, frozen. Sam was waiting for her with a smile. The hopeless pain gripped her once more.

She thought it must be easier for the dead, than for the dying.

Three days later, she told him they weren't going to have a baby. She wasn't pregnant any longer. She even said it with a smile. Like relief.

Ariel smiled at him reassuringly, but he stared at her with fear and distrust. Sam knew she was lying. Everything *would not* be okay. She knew, she felt, that things had already started falling apart.

The day things fell into place, Ariel had a panic attack. Her skin was cold, but inside, her blood was boiling. Everything inside her was tight, and she held her abdomen instinctively. She tried to breathe, but her lungs would only take in short, quick breaths. She looked up, suffocating, and the father was watching her. Already, she understood. This was not love. She had an inkling of true love, and she was sure that three and a half months from now, she would know the kind of love that hurts.

"You're still pregnant aren't you? I knew it. I damn well knew it. Shit."

He paced and then stopped, staring, one hand on his hip and the other on his head. "Sorry. Shouldn't swear or upset you. Don't want you to… miscarry or anything."

Ironic, she thought. Idiot. "Yes. I'll do it on my own, though." She had no clue how.

"No. No, I can't do that." *But he looked at her.*

"I want to."

"I want to," Sam whined. He was three and a half years old and his big brown eyes stared up at Ariel. "Please, Mommy." He smiled, a skilled manipulator.

She tried not to wonder what he would look like if he were healthy. If he hadn't had surgery and chemo. She mentally denied the fact that she would've held her ground if he hadn't been sick. It's bedtime, no more Chutes and Ladders, that's it.

"All right, Pumpkin." She smiled and kissed his nose, "One more time."

As usual, she'd miscount for him. He missed all the chutes, and she missed all the ladders. She loved to see the dimples in his cheeks when he said, "I won!" She always took second place, and Sam would look up and pat her leg, "Good job, Mommy."

In the middle of the game, as Sam bypassed his second chute for the game, he asked, still looking at the game-board, "So, I'll go to Heaven?"

They'd had this conversation before, when Sam's cat had died. *She's living in Heaven and God will take good care of her.* She smiled sadly as she recalled how Sam had asked if there were toys in heaven.

"Everyone good goes to Heaven." She replied. And there's no one better, she thought.

"But I'm going first. Before you."

Mother and son's eyes met at the same time. She stared at him blankly. Was it a contest? Did he really not understand? Did he only want to win? Or did he understand that well?

"Will I know anyone? Like people?" He glanced away and spun the spinner.

Chute or ladder? Did it matter, when she cheated anyway?

Oh my boy. My boy. She sat on her hands, digging her nails into her thighs.

"Your turn, Mommy."

She reached for the spinner. Her hand hovered over it momentarily, and she stopped. Glorious relief filled her and she smiled peacefully.

"Oh, Honey. Pumpkin." Ariel kissed the top of Sam's soft head and whispered, "I'll go with you."

Kneeling on the Chutes and Ladders game, scattering the pieces, he reached up and wrapped his arms around her neck. When he sat back again, he looked at the game and grinned mischievously.

"Guess we have to start over."

The day Sam started his life, Ariel started hers. He would sleep on her chest and she would kiss the top of his head. It was the softest, most wonderful smelling thing in the world. When he cried, she fixed it. When he smiled, she beamed. She would rock with him as he slept on her, though sweat dripped between her breasts and her arms fell asleep.

He was asleep. He was only asleep. She sat with him in the rocker. His long legs dangled awkwardly over her lap, and his head rested against her bony shoulder. As his breath became shallower, she held him tighter.

When he slipped away, her breath caught. She squeezed him with one arm as she reached for her glass of water. Before the pain could overtake her, before she could acknowledge how devastatingly sad she was, she took the pills. They'd been in her pocket for weeks now. Just in case.

Again, she wrapped her arms around his still warm body and kissed the top of his head. Tears dripped down her nose and onto his soft skin. She nuzzled his cheek and smelled his blanket. Last time. As she felt herself grow drowsy, she hoped nobody would miss her.

She double checked that Sam would not slide off her lap, her eyes flitting open and closed repeatedly.

She wouldn't deny that she lacked hope and especially faith, but it was not a lack of love that had led her to take her own life. It was a painful, pure, true love.

Ariel smiled, her last sad, lonely smile. She chose life.

Where I'm From

I am from sisters and playings,
    from "What do you want to play":
        town, train, lost-in-the-woods.
I am from the playhouse and basement,
    speeding bikes as wild horses on dirt roads, ignoring deer flies,
        from the chaos and pinkness of Barbieville and the couch-bed.
I am from microwaved bread-pizzas and fudgsicles,
    from movies in the living room with the "girls,"
        Kirsten, Samantha, Molly: living vinyl.

I am from the cousins' club,
    ballot boxes and intercoms,
        from toothpaste on doors.
I am from 4th of July newspapers,
    comics, family news, weather and games,
        from last minute editing, typewriters and copying machines.
I am from Christmas plays and practicing,
    from dark rooms and spotlight lamps,
        whistles, painted sheets and wrinkled scripts.

I am from a corner with a desk,
    from pink walls and lace curtains,
        Louisa May Alcott and Jane Austen.

I am from a blue wooden chair and handmade desk,
   shelves of books and thick, five subject notebooks,
      from mechanical pencils, reading glasses and tiny print.
I am from conversations and walks in the road,
   from Harley and Kenya,
      discussing Anna, Thomas and Runaway Trains.

I am from my childhood,
   from sisters and books,
      from happiness.

A Scene

Ghosts breathed her air. Memories cluttered her vision. Denied emotions clambered to get out. But Rebecca Jones swept them away with a blink of her darkened eyelashes, before nudging open the screen door with her elbow, hands full, and stepping into the picture that was her backyard. The cool, fall breeze was so pleasant it was almost painful as it wrapped itself seductively around her, teasing her skin with its intangibility. There was always something sad about autumn wind, and for a moment the honey and wine colored leaves that hung on the trees were blurred by the spirits she had just blown away.

The laughter of her son and nephew as they played in the leaves inspired a peaceful smile, and Rebecca relaxed as she walked toward the swinging bench in the middle of the yard where her sister was sitting, watching Sammy and Mason, both five years old and in matching hooded sweatshirts, work up a light shine of sweat on their red, smiling faces. Her eyes on the boys and her hands full of two cold cokes and two half-the-sugar juice boxes, Rebecca didn't notice the stepping stone that was a little crooked, as it always had been, and she tripped, sending the drinks flying as she freed her hands to catch herself, but there was nothing to grab onto, and she landed on her hands and knees, one coke exploding as it hit the edge of the sandbox.

"Holy cow! Did you see that?" The boys stopped what they were doing and laughed, running toward the pop that sprayed in all directions. "I can't believe it. I didn't know that could happen! Mom, can we try it with the other one?" Sammy looked at her with a huge smile on his face, knowing what a silly question it was, but still hoping she'd say yes.

Rebecca laughed, too, as she wiped away any signs of the accident from herself. "Not today. It's going to be a sticky mess already. We'll have an ant party for sure!"

"Hooray! An ant party! We love ant parties!" And the boys did a silly butt-shaking dance.

Natalie got up from her swing and danced with them for a second, looking as bright and innocent, despite having just passed her twenty fifth birthday. "We should have Dad come and redo these stones and the back patio," she said to her sister, who was already nodding, "You know he'd love to."

Their father remodeled things. It had been his job before he retired. The most interesting project he had ever worked was the renovation of their century old church. Rebecca had been sad when he decided to rip out the plush faded blue carpet that flowed down the aisles and under the pews like the sea. The blue carpet had always been there. She remembered walking down that aisle, the feel of the gray blue carpet slightly padded under her shiny white shoes as she made her first communion. Natalie, on the other hand, had been excited. She thought the church looked more romantic, the way it should have looked in the first place. Maybe the way it looked when it was first built.

But the truth is, neither one of them knew what it was like in the beginning. They couldn't have known that for one whole week, the floors were bare, raw earth; dirt, solid and cool, and that the first pastor of the church had laid the wood floors himself overnight. The people of the church had noticed for a moment, before leaving their dusty footprints on the wood floor, and then they forgot that once they had walked on the naked ground. And years would pass, and the floor would be replaced and updated, and again the people would notice for only a moment that something was different, something was off, but then they wouldn't even see the floors anymore. They were just there.

The stepping stone that had tripped Rebecca was being smashed into the ground by the heel of her outdoor slipper, as Rebecca warned the boys, "Try and stay away from this area until Grandpa comes and fixes it, ok?"

They were running back to their battle before she was even done speaking, and Rebecca felt that familiar pang. She watched them smile and laugh and play, and she wanted to drown again. She almost smiled tears when Sammy giggled as Mason stuffed leaves in the hood of his sweatshirt. They were so happy and so innocent. When they fell into the leaves, tumbling, they became one child. Joined together, laughing and squirming, you couldn't tell where one boy began and the other ended.

Sammy and Mason were often mistaken for twins. They both had sandy blonde hair, matching grins and were the same height. Mason was lankier, though, with a narrow face, while Sammy was more compact, with cheeks that dimpled. Only Rebecca and Natalie really noticed these differences in their sons; Rebecca thought Sammy was cuter, and of course Natalie felt the same about Mason.

"Becky, did you know," Natalie asked, grabbing her sister's arm and pulling her down onto the swing, "that when Sylvia Plath killed herself, she left a plate of cookies and milk in the playroom with her children? She planned her suicide so that the kids would only be alone for a little bit before the nanny arrived."

"Gee, that was thoughtful of her. Where do you learn this stuff?" Rebecca pushed away from the ground slowly, swinging gently. She imagined Sammy by himself in a playroom, wondering where his mother had gone.

"And when her husband was remarried, his second wife killed herself, too. Apparently he was a horrible husband."

"Sucks for him." What a thing to have to endure.

"But this time, this second wife, when she killed herself, she brought the kids with her. She killed them all. Well, except for the husband." Natalie pulled her knees up to her chest, letting her sister propel them forward and back on the swing.

Rebecca bit the inside of her lip, thinking briefly how Jim had once told her it was adorable when she did that. If life is so bad that you don't want to be a part of it anymore, why would you want to leave your kids in it?

"It makes sense," Natalie echoed her thoughts, which wasn't unusual. They often joked about the ESP they shared. "Otherwise, you're just leaving your kids without a mother, and in a world that you feel isn't good enough to keep living in."

Natalie let her head rest on her sister's shoulder, as a chilly breeze snuck up and tangled the loose hair at their temples, blonde strands swirling in brunette curls. The boys giggled and screamed, protected momentarily, eternally in this scene, in the beauty of innocence and mother's love.

CHAPTER 5

LISA MANNINO

A Series of Letters

July 9, 2010

Dear Superintendent,
As you begin the tedious task of recruiting candidates for the principalship in my elementary school, please consider the following character traits and required qualifications while making your selection.

First, the candidates must without doubt demonstrate positive people skills. Remember no colleague, teacher, parent or child enjoys being humiliated in the presence of their peers, as it's very demeaning to everyone involved. I realize the job of a principal can be very stressful but so is teaching. Regardless of the stress a principal may encounter throughout the day, he should always maintain a sense of calmness, dignity and respectfulness, just as I'm expected to do as a teacher with my parents and students daily.

Secondly, candidates should exhibit a real knack for communication that encompasses an elegant speaking vocabulary rather than a harsh, tell-it-like-it-is kind of language. In my opinion there is absolutely no room for rudeness, sarcasm or foul language especially in a school environment where we deal with parents and children on a daily basis.

After all, we as educators are role models for the children we teach as we shape tomorrow's world. We have one of the most important jobs in the world.

Thirdly and most importantly the candidates ought to be teacher certified with a minimum of five years of elementary teaching experience. To hire a person without a teaching certificate is reckless; by doing so you are placing the teachers and the students at a great disadvantage. Principals are the role models for teachers as teachers are for students. After all is said and done, it's the principal who sets the tone and mood of the school environment.

Last but not least, an outstanding principal in any educational setting should be able to evaluate his teachers honestly and consistently without fear of repercussions. As we strive to become polished teachers through constructive criticism from our principal it helps us to achieve high expectations.

So in closing this letter I hope you will take into consideration the above mentioned character traits and qualifications as you make your final selection.

Sincerely yours,
A Teacher's Point of View

July 16, 2010

Dear Ms. Point of View,
Thanks for your informative letter regarding the candidates for the principal that is to be assigned to your building. Your input was sincerely appreciated. I certainly will do my best as Superintendent to hire the most qualified person for your building. It's always such a challenging task to fulfill but certainly not impossible.

As I examined your letter you touched on many good points that had come to my attention from others who share your concerns. I am aware that there have been major issues that had to do with the former principal in your building who was not teacher certificated. This problem I assure you will be addressed.

I am searching for someone who has excellent people skills and who is able to project themselves in a professional manner. After all they are the role models for teachers as well as the students in the building. An interview process is currently underway at Meadow Brook Elementary School for the Administrative Principle position. I ask all teachers and staff to be patient, as this process takes time to appoint an individual with all the required credentials, as well as the experience that is to be expected of a professional educator and role model of this kind.

Sincerely,
A Superintendent's Point of View

July 23, 2010

Dear Mr. Superintendent,
I'm a student from Meadow Brook Elementary. Here are some ideas of what I think a principal should have to run our blue ribbon school. The person you hire for our school should be good with children. When I arrive to school in the morning there's nothing better than being greeted by my principal with a warm and happy smile. Kids don't like to come to school with a grumpy principal yelling at them.

Next, the person needs to be outgoing and fun. For example, I really like when the principal comes out with us during recess and plays a little kickball or helps the kindergarteners on the swings. I sure hope that the next principal will do the same.

Last but not least the new principal should be a little strict so that he or she can enforce the rules and we could learn from any mistakes that we might make.

Sincerely yours,
A Student's Point of View

Birthday Crasher

Adorable, annoying
Bossy
Confident
As adults watched in silence

Determined
Expressive, entertaining
Fluent reader
As children looked on quietly

Girly like in pink with bows
Headstrong, hyper
Ignoring boundaries
As adults bit their tongues

Jumping bean like
Know-it-all
Loud and over bearing
As children looked baffled

Manner less
Nuisance
Out-of-control
As adults began to stress

Parents are clueless
Quickly the crasher grabs
Rather rude without knowing
As children were pushed aside

Sassy like
Testy
Uncontrollable
Very vocal
As adults looked with great disbelief

Wild
eXpressive
Zipped, tight mouth everywhere, ready to blow
As the zany birthday crasher empties the wrappings all
over the beautifully manicured lawn!

CHAPTER 6

KATHY HILL

The Lighthouse Mystery

There are mysteries in my past that I don't understand. My mother is one of them. She disappeared without a trace when I was four. I am visiting my hometown for the first time in two decades, and my emotions are in turmoil. I am sitting, daydreaming, on an iron wrought garden bench on large, ancient flagstones. Behind me is the screened in sun room of the family mansion. Arched windows, iron mullions, and screens cover the spaces between the ornate brickwork. Inside, sturdy cushioned rattan furniture is placed companionably, beckoning a friend to have an iced tea or lemonade. In front of me is an enormous rock garden constructed of irregular pieces of rock. The terraced garden has creeping plants in various shades of green, white and pink slowly covering the rocks. Behind, up on a hill, is a forest of trees in their second century.

From the rock garden stepped a striking, majestic, 10-point stag. The stag looked at me and I at him and our thoughts were in sync. He was beckoning me to go on a voyage, to commence on a trek, arduous and difficult. My needs would be taken care of and I was to go immediately. I stood up and began my task.

The trail was narrow but beaten down by many footsteps before me. I walked slowly after the stag and so close I could have touched him if I reached out my hand. We came upon an ancient pile of stones and the stag disappeared, faded, vanished into the trees. I stood there and shivered, but not from cold or nerves, but rather anticipation and then I felt a soothing calm come over me. My senses quivered like the antennae on a butterfly for I knew a quest was about to be made clear to me.

I went walking around the stones and realized it was the foundation of a lighthouse. I puzzled over the distance I was from the water of a great lake. Suddenly the silence was split by the screech of a seagull. I looked overhead at the tops of ancient oaks, pines and maples; gnarled branches reaching towards the sun sensing the glimpse of a lake.

"Why was I here?" I wondered.

My toe caught on something as I was ambling around and I looked down to see a rusty metal ring. Spying a shovel shaped rock, and a brush-like branch of twigs I retrieved them and slowly began to extricate my find. Slowly, careful not to crumble more any existing metal, I worked for what seemed like hours. After tediously brushing, digging and unearthing in inch layers I was able to pull out a metal box with ornate designs of shells and seahorses patterned over the top and sides.

Hot, sweating, and scratching mosquito bites, I carefully placed the box on a large upended tree trunk. I brushed my damp bangs from my eyes and examined the box. It was exquisite despite the crusty rust dusted over the surface. An overwhelming feeling to rescue someone came over me.

"Odd", I thought and shook my head to clear it. I took a deep breath and placed both hands on the lid with my fingers curved under the lip. Pressing and pulling gently I moved the lid side to side and eased it open.

The smell of Bee Balm, cinnamon, and lemon, drifted out of the box. I savored the scent inhaling deeply several times because it had been my mother's favorite. Peering inside the box I first saw a black, rusted, three pronged, old style key. The key was actually quite large, like a key to a castle turret door from a fairy tale. Nestled in a corner were tiny emerald frog earrings. I gently brushed away whitish dust on the emeralds off with my fingertips to reveal tiny gold eyes peering at me.

I turned my attention to the bottom padding. I could see lines etched on it. Slowly easing edge and sides free, I pulled up the molding leather, bringing it up in one piece. I felt a rustle and it distracted me so I looked up. The stag was close, silent, and regarding me with his deep brown eyes. I turned my attention back to the map, for certainly it looked like a map now to me with lines, symbols and words inscribed on it.

Right away, I recognized the symbol for a lighthouse where I now stood and saw the wavy lines for water at the farthest edge of the map from the lighthouse. If the ovals represented paces then there were almost 100 of them from the lighthouse to the lake. Just the realization of the proximity of the water allowed me to scent fish, waves, and sand. Inhaling deeply I felt compelled to walk to the water's edge.

I walked with the chest in my arms, quickly and with purpose, guided by the roaring of the waves and crying seagulls. My heartbeat quickened with excitement. On the beach, I stood barefoot in the warm sand, and saw sea oats and the gentle rise of sand dunes. There were deer prints on the sand and determining which direction they were headed I tracked them. They abruptly ended at an inlet hidden by surrounding dunes.

Stumbling and falling, I managed to keep the chest safe. Nevertheless, I landed on my seat. I blinked and looked around, still sitting, and saw a row- boat hidden in the grasses. Something I could not have seen if I had remained upright. I got up and pulled the boat to the beach. The boat was seaworthy and equipped with oars and a backpack full of water, energy bars and a hat!

"Hmm" I thought, "One if by land. Two if by sea," Paul Revere's famous saying reverberated in my head, "Now what?"

I looked long and hard across the endless lake, seeing no shore, nothing to interrupt the landscape of the waves. Discouraged I sat down and closed my eyes. Looking again to the horizon where the earth's curves block the view of beyond, I suddenly stood up. I saw a vertical mark in the water. Peering, squinting, stretching my vision like a rubber band, I discovered a lighthouse. Thin, miniscule, far away, it was there and I knew where I was to go next. The sun was beating down on my head.

"OK" I said to myself, "time to carry on."

I put on the hat, the life jacket, drank some water, and ate a granola bar. I pushed the boat into the water where it floated gently and hopped in. Steadily gaining rhythm and power, I started to row toward the pinpoint lighthouse.

I'm cautious by nature and when I started rowing through the waves I stopped and glided a bit to think. I'm twenty four, five foot three with strawberry blond hair. Meaning I am not big, strong, or reckless. I am a smaller person, a female. I know my limitations, as I have been independent since I was a little girl. My unpredictable behavior, following the stag, puzzled me. Usually I'm the one to pull my friends back from some crazy impulsive adventure with reasons to be cautious.

As I puzzled, a wave splashed over the boat side and hit me in the face. I awoke from my reverie to look up and see dark clouds scurrying my way. Putting the pedal to the metal, my back muscles into my rowing, I increased my speed. Actually, I couldn't believe how much I increased my speed, and I stopped rowing. The boat kept moving!

The boat glided up the beach, scraping on the sand. The sun appeared and I closed my eyes feeling the heat again, this time on my face. When I opened my eyes the sky was dark and I was looking into a shaft of light, a lighthouse beam, beckoning me, pulling me, enticing me, towards it.

I walked into the beam of the Fresnel lens so far away from where I had started, and I thought of my mother. It had been 20 years since she had left, but her fragrance seemed to be misting the air. I thought wistfully of her garden, and a memory came to me as clear as the day it happened so many years ago. It dawned on me that this memory was the answer to a thousand questions.

On the first day of spring we had seen so many flowers bloom in the year that mother and I gazed over the flower garden because the beauty was all over and it was due to the bright sunlight of spring. The snow had been melting since Sunday. Landscapes and gardens were awash in color and the sky, gray and cloudy had become brilliant and blue. The light was so bright Mother had to squint to look around her immense garden, and she nearly missed the colorful creature in the back corner under the trees. She had to peer closely to see it was a small elf, a very small elf sitting up and holding a sparkling treasure in his hands. I was there, holding my mother's hand crying, pulling her back so hard that when she wrenched away to go to the tiny man. I fell backwards hitting my head on the wrought iron garden bench.

The present commanded my attention and I realized I was standing in front of a weathered, arched oak door with a very familiar looking keyhole. I was still clutching the chest and I put it down and retrieved the key inside. The emerald frog earrings fell out and as they hit the ground I heard fairy chimes. Bending over and picking them up the gold eyes sparkled at me and I almost dropped them. My fist firmly closed around the shining earrings, I used the other hand to insert the key and open the door. The door groaned open. I was at the foot of a curving, patterned, spiral staircase. It was dark inside with the beacon far above me, but the earrings glowed enough to light my way.

My longing for my mother unexpectedly became so strong I could barely breathe. Inhaling a deep, cleansing, breath I continued my incline and stopped at a door that was slightly ajar. Pushing through, I gasped at what I saw. A fantasy bower of Bee Balm blossoms surrounded a bed and on the bed was my mother. Young, pink-cheeked, breathing softly with her auburn hair spread out on the pillow. Tiptoeing closer with tears spilling down my cheeks, so many warm memories flooded me.

The earrings were chiming, jumping, and burning in my hand. Gently a magical lilting voice said "to break the charm put the emeralds where they rightly belong."

Tenderly locating the pierces in her earlobes, I hung the tiny golden amphibians. My mother's eyes slowly opened and she smiled. A tear trickled down her cheek and she raised her arms in that oh-so familiar way. Weeping, I enfolded myself in her arms.

Aah Camp!

Sleeping bags
Mosquito netting and frame
Bug spray, flashlight
Labeled underwear
Platform tents with thick canvas wall that roll up and let the breezes in
Dining hall duty, songs and chants
Announcements, Announcements, Annowowcements!

Raking seaweed to make a beach
Horseback riding in circles
Sneaky hikes after hours
Snipe hunts
Latrines that wrinkle your nose
Singing 'Give Me Oil for My Lamp,' 'Canadian Wilderness,'
At the top of our little girl voices
Plastic and gum wrapper lanyards
Braided friendship bracelets, monkey fists, and god's eyes
Rest time to read comics my mom and sister sent me
Writing twelve page letters to Gretchen
Poison Ivy, mosquito bites, dirty fingernails and Calamine lotion
Showers open to the sky
Badges, knots, canoes, rowboats, swimming lessons
Queen of my tent
Queen of my camp
Queen of me!

Tea with Jamison

I was teaching at a Title One school in a first grade classroom when I met Jamison. Jamison was bright, wiggly, little, and full of energy, the kind that makes teaching difficult at times. I had conversations with him; he was always telling me things and asking about my life and I must have mentioned that I liked to drink tea with my friends. Well, he decided to invite me over to his house to visit. I put him off by telling him I was busy, had to get home etc, but he kept persisting. Finally, I said that if he brought a note home from his mother I would come and visit. I knew they lived in a project duplex, and I was concerned his mother might be ashamed to have a teacher visit. In addition, I knew that my house was not always ready and clean to receive visitors, and I did not want to drop in unannounced. I also worried that the other teachers would disapprove.

Well, his mom came to school to tell me it was ok, so I agreed on a date after school. I followed him home (a whole half a block) in my car and noted several older people on their front porches watching me.

I really did not want to be the talk of the neighborhood, but a promise is a promise.

Jamison proudly led me into his home and offered me a seat at the kitchen table. He gave me an ashtray, and asked if I would like to smoke. I said no. He asked his mom to sit with me and she declined saying he should sit down, as I was his guest. We sat in silence for a few minutes. Then I said that if he had invited me over for tea, he should get us some tea. He jumped up, climbed up on the counter to fetch a mug and a packet of hot chocolate. Then he sat down. I said that when one invited someone over for tea, one should have some himself. So he jumped up, climbed back up on the counter, and got himself a mug and a packet of hot chocolate mix. He sat down again with a wide grin and looked at me.

I said that the tea would taste better if we added some hot water to it. He jumped up again, turned in the hot water in the sink and filled our mugs carefully. He brought spoons and we mixed our hot chocolate.

He was quiet for a long time and then said, "Now what do we do?"

I said, "Well, we drink our tea and talk to each other. "

I asked him questions like what did he usually do after school and who were his friends. He asked me about my life after school and we had a pleasant conversation. Then he jumped up; Jamison was not a child who made slow movements or who could sit still for a longtime, and asked me if I would like to see his house. I looked at his mother, who was patiently sitting in the living room, and she nodded that it would be ok.

He showed me the bathroom and said that was where he cleaned his teeth every morning when he was getting ready to go to school. He then took me to his own room, which I could see he was intensely proud of. He then proceeded to open all his drawers and show me his clothes and his one toy. He even showed me where he kept all his papers from school. He had one picture on the wall that he pointed out with pride as he explained he had drawn it himself.

He then took me to the backyard and showed me his climbing tree. Jamison told me a story about the mean old lady on the other side of the fence. I asked why she was mean and what she did to him and his friends, and he related how they took apples from her yard sometimes and teased her when they scrambled back over the fence. She yelled at them, he said.

Jamison lived in a duplex the size of my living room. He had only two or three changes of clothing. One beat up cheap child's computer toy was all I saw, yet he spoke with pride and admiration of his home and his life. I knew him well; he was an active child preferring to run around and play with friends as opposed to sitting and playing quietly. His mother was silent the whole visit busying herself with a toddler and folding laundry. He told me with no emotion that his dad was a good-for- nothing and I, without looking at his mother, could imagine her wincing, and I would have if my child had told a teacher my personal business.

I was touched and filled with love for Jamison and admiration for a mother who raised her son with such love that he was proud enough of his life to invite his teacher home for tea. I wish more children would invite me home for tea.

Thoughtful Alphabet Poem

Alluring Bee-balm
Charming Dogwood
Elegant Forsythia
Gigantic Hollyhocks
Iceplant Jubilee

Killer Larkspur

Manic Noisy Oleander

Poppies Quilting

Restful Snapdragons

Trillium Under Violets

Wisteria

Exotic Yearning Zinnias

A Beachy Celebration

We were hot, sticky and sweaty, and right by the lake. My daughter and I were headed to the big beach to swim. The water was warm. The waves were getting bigger. Storm clouds were overhead so we didn't take towels or shoes to the beach—no need. The water was so soothing to my sunburn. We dunked, swam up and under like porpoises. Then came the rain—no thunder or lightening—just a fast and furious stinging rain. We lifted our arms up laughing because we were already wet! Dunking under to avoid the pelting rain, running, tripping and splashing. Dark skies to one side, sun on the other and then it stopped. We'd had a moment, my daughter and I, a glorious memorable, unique moment—where we raised our arms up in pure joy.

I Am From

I am from jumping off the front porch at 1915 Cresthill,
From snowstorms so high we tunneled through,
From marching the length of my backyard and throwing away my 'Blanky'

I am from the drop of water that ripples on and on,
From Girl Scout camp, horseback riding, swimming in weeds and bug
    juice,
From Nancy Drew, Betsy, Dorothy Gale, and Katie Scarlet,
I am from fresh raspberries and feta cheese at Eastern Market,
From stuck on the top of the monkey bars at Kindergarten Round-up,

From standing on the piano bench in class proudly counting out loud
   to one hundred,
I am from napping on a rug, reading aloud and imagining greatness,
From riding a two-wheeler, burying treasure and unlimited possibilities
From teaching and reveling in childhood mysteries and imagination

How Do You Decide?

How do you decide when to push and when to pull?
When to console and when to shake it off?
When to quit and when to try?
When to correct and when to praise?
When to advise and when to listen?
When to question and when to affirm?
When to challenge and when to step back?
When to guide and when to thwart?
When to 'coddle' and when to 'tough-love'?
How do you decide to react or reflect when you are a teacher?
(A poem inspired after reading 'My Mother's Gravy' by Bobby Ann
Starnes)

Writing Wisdom

Writing Wisdom is letting yourself write. It's letting it all come out
from your thoughts down your arm into the pen and onto the paper.
It's letting yourself imagine, and no thought is too outlandish or silly,
because stories and essays start with a thought. It's letting yourself block
out all the criticisms you have ever heard or thought of about writing.
Writing Wisdom is letting yourself realize that your stories are as unique
as you, no one has the same thoughts or experiences at the same time,
that is, what makes your writing interesting. It's your voice, your take,
your imagination, your life, and your conversations with all the authors
you have ever read. Writing Wisdom is lessons and getting it all down in
creative forms. It's letting yourself feel without any censure and letting
that feeling flow into your writing.

Seven-Word Poem

The stopover
In the crotch
Of the overpass
was a special place.
Scents of
Fresh baked cinnamon rolls
Were as strong
As the swelling notes
Of a Bach Chorale
Drifting in the breeze.
Smoke-like fog
Swirled around
The statues
Of still remembered
Nobility,
Peace permeated
the air.
Cinnamon, Stopover, Overpass, Bach
Chorale, Smoke, Nobility, Crotch

CHAPTER 7

MARY MURPHY

Books

Books are treasures! They allow us to travel to worlds unknown from under a shade tree, sipping lemonade on a hot summer day. Walking into a library feels serene and calm with the enduring strength of books all around. It is the place where dreams filling the pages of books come alive.

Treasures
Worlds unknown
Library
Serene
Calm
Pages Dream
Enduring strength
Surround

Writing Process and Product

It is the writer that is changed by instruction and conferring. If we are to sustain the writer and nurture growth over time, our focus must be on the writer – on the process in creating a learning environment which promotes writing. We must lead the writer to develop the art of metacognition – to reflect and self-evaluate and set goals. Growth over time will flourish given the support and awareness of the next step. What is the writer on the verge of doing? What does the piece reveal about the writer as a writer? It is the teacher, in the role of coach, who will serve to support, scaffold, and lead the writer by a nudge in the right direction. The writing conference is the "information in a tip." In the role of coach, the teacher needs to be able to present that "next step" to the child. Writing is a process in that the writer continues to apply all that came before to future pieces. The product should not be compromised in this process. The goal is to produce great writing.

Rules to Live By

(an ABC poem)
Always be careful
Do everything fashionably
Guard hearts impeccably
Judge kindly
Live more naturally
Open presents quickly
Reserve some time
Understand very well
Extend your zoom!

STAR

Scorching sun

Penetrating fireball

Hazy veil

Halting movement

Yearning for respite

Nature's heirloom

The ABCs of Mr. Buster

(My Golden Retriever Friend)
Always in trouble
Big black polar bear nose
Curious and caring and cuddly
Daring determined demeanor
Engaging energy
Frisky friend
Grinning golden gift
Happy and handsome
Inventive and insistent
Jolly jowls
Kinglike and kind
Long lolling tongue
Magnetic personality
Noble and nurturing
Offspring of Ollie Oops
Powerful pearly white choppers
Quick as a lick
Regal and royal
Smile from ear to ear
Tenacious traveler

Unwavering love
Voki voice
Wavy curls which beg to be touched
Xoxo
Your best friend
Zany with zillions of kisses!

I'm Going to Love Them

By Buster B. Dogg Murphy

I'm going to assume you've heard of me. Obviously, you're reading these words, so I'm pretty sure I've done something to attract your attention. And if not, then prepare to have your socks knocked off because I am THE Buster. I'm tough, I'm gruff, I'm rude and crude, but I'll be the best friend you'll ever have in the world. They call me big and bad, but scratch my stomach and I'll turn into a canine Galahad. I'm noble and sturdy, strong and trustworthy, but never forget for a second I'll gladly roll around in the mud with you and get dirty. So you get the picture with my personality; I'm a warm teddy bear who digs wearing rhinoceros skin.

I'm a golden lion, as long as I am tall; I've got eyes like smoldering opals and a tongue so long it drags on the ground when I'm thirsty. I've got velvet ears that can hear better than you can see, and a shotgun nose that can smell all types of scents you can't. I love to run and jump and to slide and play; I love biting and rolling in the grass on hot summer days. But I don't really want to bore you with the details; no, I've come to explain how I came to live with Mary and Steve and Sean, and geez, did I luck out with them; they give me anything I want!

One day when I was very young, still living with my brother and mother, I awoke to a beam of light from the sun. The door had opened, and I couldn't believe it, here came these three bizarre but loveable humans! I knew immediately I liked them, they smelled so kind and sweet and their personalities, I thought, just couldn't be beat!

I was very small then, not all the behemoth I am now, so I was easily lifted by Mary up and out, and as she held me I knew without a doubt, this one! This is the family I want to live with, I began to deeply shout! And then Steve played with me on the floor, jumping and clapping and hooting, and I knew all the more, that I had definitely lucked out when these people came through the door. I played with Sean on the stairs and knew I had found the companion with which I could always joke around!

Eventually we all agreed, and I was off with them gee, was I happy! Into what I would later learn was called The Car, a strange device with wheels for paws! I climbed up and crawled into a crevice made between the seat and the back windshield. To my surprise, my new friends thought this a strange feat, boy I thought, they haven't seen nothin' yet, wait till I show'em all my circus tricks, I bet they'll think that's incredibly neat!

Arriving at my new house, I felt strangely calm. It was like I had been here before; I felt so at home. I loved it here, the air vents and crevice spaces, the warm, comfortably feeling of complete love and the introduction of new food, housing some rather exquisite tastes.

I like to think to myself on warm summer evenings, as I feel the wind caress my golden fur and I lay on the patio munching on a grade-A chewstick quietly, that somehow all of this is destiny. That it is most definitely with these loving, caring, kind people I am meant to be, and I know that they will always take wonderful care of me. And that as much of a problem dog I can be, I hope that they know I will always shower them with love and kisses, joy and fond wishes, even if it comes out a little "ruff!" Because love is the key, and when I feel frustrated with one of them, what do I do? I think to myself in a canine fashion, licking my chops and concentrating with that single minded dog driven passion, "I'm gonna love them!"

My Favorite Day of the Week

As I slowly awake, fighting the urge to sink back into that dreamy state called "Without a Care in the World," I feel the cool, cottony sheets envelope me. Shifting from side to side while burying my head in the soft, white, fluffy pillow, I smell the sweet fragrance of jasmine floating through the open window. I feel the warmth of the sun with its beams of light casting shadows of geometric design surround me. The aroma of freshly fried bacon and the image of French toast dipped in sweet maple syrup awaken me. Saturday is the best!

Where I'm From

I am from freshly picked raspberries from the lone raspberry bush outside my bedroom window

I am from VE-94681 and 15611 Fairmont and streetcars running down Gratiot

I am from "Do Your Best, Mary" and weekends spent learning how to cheat at cards with my Grandpa McDonald

I am from "The Lone Ranger Rides Again" and Shirley Temple

I am from pickled herring and aged Colby cheese wrapped in red wax

I am from dancing around the coffee table to the tunes of "Poppy the Puppy" and "How Much is that Doggie in the Window?"

I am from "Red Rover, Red Rover, Won't You Come Over?" and my dad's gentle reminder to come home when the street lights come on

I am from an empty house after school, and Mrs. Parr making tea and toast while watching Danny Thomas

I am from red, juicy sweet cherries pulled from the cherry tree standing tall above my swing set where I penciled my daily schedule

I am from a black and white taffeta dress splashed with mud on a dirt road on a rainy Easter Sunday

I am from my Grandpa Pohlman stealing green olives off my plate while visiting in his trailer cabana

I am from wonderings about my mom and my dad's tears when visiting my mom's grave

I am from the nightly Choo-Choo train dropping me in bed and

I am from "Now I Lay Me Down to Sleep."

Loss

I just learned today
My friend has died
Where did the time go?
It was just last week
I sent a just right card
Picturing a near future time
We'd share laughs and memories.

She was just diagnosed
Lung and bone cancer her enemies
Just one month ago
Who would have thought
She would lose the battle
Just four weeks later.

Having retired just one year ago
Where is the justice?
Death feels so dark, indifferent, and vast
A feeling of cold steel bars
Isolating friends forever.

Now it is too late to get together
To share laughs of times past.
The lesson has been learned:
HONOR THE URGENCY OF TIME.
Be keenly aware of its swiftness.
Death has come like a thief in the night
Stealing away my friend forever.

She has joined the angels in heaven
Where new friends will be made
Someday I hope to see her again
Where she is free of pain
Free to share laughs and memories.

Until then I will hold her in my heart
A respected friend with incredible strength.
There is one less flower in Earth's garden.
Our loss has become Heaven's gain.

Chapter 8

ANN DENISON

You Can Call Me Ann

When I was born on September 9, 1978, my biological mother named me Alberta Ann Elsberry. It was actually much later in my life that I realized that this was my first name because it is not the name I have now. I found out that my name was Alberta from my adopted parents, the Denisons. I have always been thankful that it was not my permanent name for life. Needless to say my life has been very eventful, and my name is just the beginning of the story.

As long as I can remember I have always answered to Ann. This was the name I was given when I lived with my foster parents, the Whannels, and this is the name I kept when I was adopted in September 1981 by the Denisons. I have to say that I have never liked my name. I always wanted to have a different name, but the older I get the more I realize that Ann suits me quite perfectly. I have always been told that my parents kept the name Ann because that is what my foster parents named me, but I guess there was a toss up between Ann Marie Denison or Ann Elizabeth Denison. I ended up with Ann Marie Denison and share the same middle name with my biological sister, Tina, who was also adopted with me.

The name Ann means "graceful" or full of grace, as I learned from a name card my mom bought me years ago. Ann is usually considered an old name, or a name that was popular many decades ago. I have always thought of the name being sort of a conservative and very simple name. That certainly describes me. I have always lived a simple life. I never felt like I needed a lot of things to make me happy. I was raised in a very religious and conservative home. My dad was a minister for 30 years so, in other words, I was a pastor's kid.

I have never answered to other versions of Ann even though various people have tried calling me them. One name that stands out to me was "Annie-Get-Your-Gun." I remember a man from my church camp used to call me that. I always thought it was funny even though I had never heard of it before. I have also been called "Annabelle" and "Annie" by my band teacher. I never really cared for those names either. In addition, my aunt Maxine has always called me "Ann Marie" as long as I have known her. Most people call me Ann, and that is what I like, and no, it is not with an e!

My Adopted Mom "Nancy"

Amazing, Blessing
Clever, Devoted
Elegant, Faithful
Generous, Hilarious
Intuitive
Just, Kind, Listener
Multi-talented, Nurturing
Open-minded, Patient
Quiet, Role model
Sacrificial, Trustworthy
Understanding, Virtuous
Wise, Xoxo's
Youthful, Zest

My Family Trip to Florida

It's 5 am and we're up. Mom calls me. "Ann, time to get up." "Ugh!" I say. I was never a morning person, and I am about the grouchiest person I know at the start of a day. We were getting ready to go on vacation to Florida, a trip I had wanted to come for weeks. I thought about all the fun that was awaiting me. But then I thought about the drive. We were driving a long way. Days of being packed into a van was not my way of enjoying a vacation. Nevertheless, I got up, dressed, and showed my face to the family who was very busy getting things around for the trip. Soon we would be in Florida. I was going to see my sister whom I had not seen for a year. Excitement filled my veins. The next thing I know we were packed and off. I anticipated the beautiful beaches, swimming in the hotel pool, and visiting Disney World, Epcot, and Wet-n-Wild. I looked forward to looking in stores, gift shops, and more. After all, I had been saving those pop cans for several months before. I was proud of myself for the money I had raised, and I was going to enjoy every minute of spending it too. Looking back this was the best trip I have ever had!

The Life of My Sister Tina

Tina was the name given to my biological sister I was adopted with in 1981. Tina is four years older than me so she was seven, and I was three when we were adopted. Although she was four years older, she was only three years ahead of me in school. She had to repeat kindergarten. I always remember Tina as being pretty in her own way. She had brown hair, blue eyes, and a beautiful smile that showed her nearly perfect white teeth. After all she never had to have braces; those pretty teeth were hers. Although we are connected through our bloodline with the same mother and looked very similar in the face with high cheek bones, we are very different in many ways. As children, many people would get us mixed up, thinking I was my sister and she was me due to the way we looked. I would commonly be called Tina and her Ann. It always seemed funny to me since she was always much taller and her build was overall much different than mine.

Tina and I always spent a lot of time together as most children do. I can remember riding bikes with her around town, going to the library, and spending a great deal of time at the park. One of her favorite things to do was braid my hair, a skill she taught herself. She was great at French braids; however, she always braided my hair so tight I felt like my eyebrows were going to fall out. My dad was a pastor at a church, and we worked together cleaning it to earn our weekly allowance. We enjoyed attending summer kids' camp and family camp with our parents. We both had many friends that we kept in touch with for years. Tina and I always went to our weekly piano lessons and both played an instrument, Tina the trumpet and I played the clarinet. My parents always wanted us to be musically inclined. Even though we were given a lot of blessings with being part of the Denison family, it seemed that Tina was always the oddball, the loner, the rebellious one, the one with her own ideas.

From the time I was old enough to learn about Tina and I and the adoption, Tina always seemed unsettled about it. She would quite frequently ask me about our mother and always expressed a deep desire to find her. It was almost like she couldn't move on with her life without finding her.

As my sister grew older and got into high school, she started changing. I wish I could say for the better, but it wasn't, it was for the worse. She constantly got into arguments, usually with my dad, but also with others in the family. Tina was always easily manipulated and because she wanted to fit in, she made choices she knew were wrong. She commonly was known to smoke on the corner at school during lunch, and she got involved with these men who were in my opinion a waste of time. All I know is she hung around what I called the wrong crew and she became a different person. She never wanted to follow the rules at home and seemed to think that our house was a revolving door in which she could come and go as she pleased.

I believe that some of Tina's unsettledness and her low self-esteem came from the fact that she struggled a great deal in school. Nothing ever came easy for her. I can remember my mom helping her night after night on her school work. I always remember feeling like if it wasn't for my mom's help, my sister never would have made it through school. Even though school was difficult for her, Tina loved to read and write.

She spent hours in her room listening to her music and reading book after book, at least one book every day.

After high school Tina continued to make bad choices. One year later she got pregnant by a man who she had been in relationship with for awhile. She supposedly met him while working at Meijers. My parents were not happy to hear that she was pregnant, but they knew something was bound to happen since they were living together, against my parents' conservative wishes. In fact, I even remember that Tina didn't tell my mom; my mom just knew. After Alexander was born, my parents tried to convince my sister that she needed to get her life together and encouraged her to move home, and they even went as far as helping her to get involved with a Christian organization for single moms that would help her raise Alex and go to school. Tina had made the decision to go, and my parents got her packed and ready, and she backed out the day before she was supposed to leave. Needless to say my parents were rather frustrated, but they also realized it was her choice. Now looking back, that was probably the changing point in her life. She had a chance to make something of her life and she bailed.

Tina always loved children. In high school she was a student at the career tech center for two years. She worked with young children in a daycare setting. She loved it and did very well according to her teachers. In fact, my parents even encouraged her to finish the program there. She only needed to be in the program for one more year and she would have earned an associate's degree in child development. This obviously never came to fruition, another opportunity down the drain.

Over the next four years, Tina did end up getting married, just a couple of months before the second child came, and had two more children, Caleb and Courtney, who were eleven months apart in age. Eventually her marriage ended due to her husband being abusive to her and the children, his unfaithfulness, and because of their constant fighting, which was causing a great deal of stress on the children. The children were put in a foster home for a year and due to their unsuccessful marriage counseling, the children were taken away and adopted out. All sides felt bad about the situation especially my parents and Tina. When my parents were asked to adopt the children, they said no due to the fact that they were near retirement and felt they were too old to take on three young children.

Sometime later Tina started attending AA, which is where she met her second husband, Jerry. Although Jerry had been an alcoholic for years, Tina married him despite the fact that he was 20 years older than her. She is currently still married to him now, but there have been a ton of problems in their marriage. Tina and Jerry were pregnant several times even though they only had two children together. As with the first marriage, the children were taken away due to her record that resulted from her first marriage. Soon after they got married, Jerry resorted back to his alcoholic ways, and Tina has paid for it greatly. Much of what I know about my sister over the past ten years has come from conversations with my mom. Tina rarely calls the family unless she needs something. It was common for us to go for months without hearing from her. Even when she does call, she ends up getting mad or defensive and either cusses at you or hangs up the phone. As she has gotten older, I have seen less and less of her. She claims it is because they have no money, which is probably true since they have both lived off the state collecting disability due to their issues for years. After all, neither one of them has had a job since they have been married.

What a life.

Now that I am an adult I guess I have mixed feelings about my sister. Sometimes I think I should feel obligated to stay in touch with her because she is my real sister, but I don't feel that strong urge to connect with her. A year and a half ago, Tina did track down the whereabouts of my mom. We always knew she was living in Iowa somewhere in a state home. Sometime after that she sent me a current picture of our mom through email. I really didn't have much feeling about looking at that picture except that I remember feeling she was ugly. I have spent a great deal of time working to make something of my life and not take the path that my mom and sister took. In fact I found it interesting that my mom got very emotional finding out that I had become a teacher. Tina wanted me to call our mom and talk with her to get caught up as she called it, and because I never had a desire, I never did, and it made my sister quite upset with me. My entire life Tina was always jealous of me. She would always make comments about how pretty I was, how successful I was with becoming a teacher and getting my degrees, getting a job and having my own place. Maybe this is why I don't feel that I can connect with her. My life is very different from hers. I would always find it funny that whenever I dated a guy she always wanted to know about it. She liked being the older sister as she claimed her job was to protect me from them. She always told me never to put up with anything from a man, even though she settled for a lot.

Currently Tina is in jail where she has been since last March. She told us the story many times as to why she was in jail, but the story changed every time. First it was, "I am going to be in overnight," then that turned into three months, and now she says it might be January before she will be out. Of course it started with the nightly fight she had with Jerry after he had too much alcohol, and then you can pretty much fill in the blanks as to what happened from there. It usually resulted in one or the other calling the police to break up their argument. I guess I hope that jail will help her to put things into perspective in her life. It brought tears to my eyes when I read a letter she wrote to my parents from jail. You could really tell that she had done a lot of soul searching. I just hope for her sake she realizes that her life is heading in the wrong direction and she finally does something about it once and for all.

Obviously I can't predict the future so I don't know what is coming next for Tina in her life. I do hope that someday she realizes her value and that she is here on earth for a purpose and that purpose was not to be miserable and upset every day. I do hope that she can learn to take care of herself and make better choices, whether that be seeing a therapist, getting a job, or going back to school, which is something she has tried to do several times. All in all, I hope she finds happiness and realizes that there are people out there who do care for her, and I hope most of all that she knows deep inside her heart that she is loved.

Where I'm From

I am from corn fields and trees, running frequently in the woods,
I am from winning tons of medals and running many races.
I am from eating lots of pasta, grilled steaks and burgers,
I am from eating fresh fruits and veggies
right out of our gigantic garden.
I am from a religious home where faith was valued,
I am from if anything is worth doing, it's worth doing right.
I am from one set of parents and raised by another,
I am from a home that helped me become the woman I am today.
I am from riding bikes, playing at the park,
and going to summer camps,
I am from playing with Ms. Beasley, blocks, and cabbage patch dolls.
I am from playing clarinet, choir, and piano lessons,
I am from practicing daily.
I am from many heartaches, love, and maturing,
I am from hours of communication about life and learning.
I am from graduating from college, masters, and loans,
I am from hard work pays off motto at my home.
Thank God for experiences throughout my life
It's made the person I am striving to be!

CHAPTER 9

CAROLYN NEWELL

First Day

My eyes are dashing all around,
My mind is racing,
My stomach has butterflies,
My palms are sweaty,
My foot taps,
I'm anxious,
I'm excited!

Will I find the right room?
Where will I sit?
Who will I meet?
What will I be doing?
Did I bring the right things?
I'm anxious,
I'm excited!
A New Day, A New School!

While I Wait

I
Meditate
Contemplate
Fabricate
Create
Calculate
Deliberate
Speculate
Anticipate
Debate
Celebrate
Exaggerate
Exasperate
Communicate
Delegate
Manipulate
Appreciate

New Discoveries

We pulled up to a white house with a long driveway. I had my dollar from Grandma in hand. I'm so excited my seat belt is unhooked the moment the car stops.

As I wait for Mom to open the door I am looking everywhere.

I see sparkly glass and big speakers- Dad might like those!

I run toward the garage then stop. I'm supposed to wait for Mom. There is so much to look at.

Dust sparkles are floating in the sun light through the trees. The garage is cooler than being out in the sun.

The tables are full of kitchen stuff, towels, glass and things a little boy doesn't find too interesting.

It is the things under the table that I'm interested in. There's an airplane of metal. Oh, the number is 2 and I only have 1.

There are games, puzzles, round things called records, Mom tells me, and stuffed animals. This is better than a toy store!

There is a box of cards with rubber bands around piles. I start looking, baseball and hockey players, cars, animals including dinosaurs. I find one that is a dog. I turn the card over and around. It's with a group marked 20 cents but I don't want the other cards with it.

Mom is asking about a bowl that is funny shaped and painted with flowers.

I keep looking, putting the card on top of its pile.

Under the other table I find a puzzle of cars with 50 pieces. Oh, a small plane for only 25 cents – all red and plastic. There are marbles and games. Oh, a ball for 10 cents-red my color. There is a stuffed dinosaur. My last one got run over by Dad's lawn mower. I hadn't put it away and dad didn't see it- stuffing flew everywhere.

Mom asks me if I am ready. I pop up and show her my treasures. We add puzzle, plane and ball 85cents. Not enough money left for the cards.

I got brave and say, "I only want the dog card- see this one on top." The nice owner says, "It's yours".

I gave her my dollar and she put my puzzle, plane, ball, and card in a bag and handed it to me. Then she gave me a nickel and a dime. I got money back.

Mom paid for her bowl and took my hand. I skipped to the car with dust sparkles dancing around us.

This was the first time I had fun at a Garage Sale!

Charlie's Retell
Reflection and reminder

Just this Wednesday I was sitting at the dinner table with our just two year old grandson. He is developing his communication skills. Perhaps because I am an early childhood educator and grandmother, I have been able to take the time to observe his language development. He has gone through sounds, through pointing with adults anxious to give him words, then saying words he has heard. He loves animals and will tell you the name of the pictures and models he sees.

In June the first sentence was "Come here, Ma Ma". Wow, words together to make yes! that first thought known! The biggest excitement and delight came to me as Charlie was what I thought babbling in sentence length and looking at me intently. I heard "Giant feet" repeated several times then finally the word "water". My husband said first he didn't understand, then as I clarified the speech, imagine my surprise when my husband said- oh he's telling you the story of a program we had seen today. So my husband looked at our grandson and said, "That's right, the giant had his feet in the water and blocked the fish." The look on my grandson's face was like "Yes, you got it," and mine was elated surprise- he did a retell and we had our first conversation! My grandson felt vindicated.

I'm always awed by how the human mind coordinates and progresses with learning. Storytelling is one of the leads to writing. Our little ones are truly wondrous. The processes and learning constantly going on is amazing.

ABC Poem

Aerobic ballet
Creative exercise form
Good healthcare
Isometric, jumping jacks
Kicks, lunges
Muscles
Natural oxygen pull-ups
Quick running
Squats transforming unbalanced veins
Experiencing yoga zealously.

Frustrated

The phrase in my head
Keeps sliding into oblivion as I wake
Oh where is that great line, poem
Thought?

New Habit

I still my mind
Noise removed, quiet place
No multitasking here
Time to write.
Purely Joyful Experience
Do Not Disturb

I am from...

I am from Guerlain and Old Spice,
Antiques, the smell of old books, and seven sets of china.
I am from Grandpa's lap and National Geographic and
Dilly Dallies on Grandma's porch.
I am from dinner conversations and trying to sit still.

I am from skinned knees and reading high in the willow tree,
Lilac bushes, bee stings, and spending days outside.
I am from conquering roller skates, bikes, and climbing,
New friends, car sickness, and alone time.
I am from Army brat and Navy wife, college graduate, and professional.

I am from Nancy Drew, Erma Bombeck, Agatha Christie, and Garrison
    Keillor
Mystery, humor, and professional reads.
I am from Mom, Grandmother, and Daughter
A team player and a good friend.
I am from Luther League, Camp Counselor, Sorority Sister, and
    Educator
I am from "Do your personal best!" and "Turn out the lights!"

A Small Moment

It is the last day of the school year-a half day and things are moving as planned and expected. The class made pancakes and a huge fruit bowl to share with the 5th grade Buddies. The room was cleaned and the good byes were said to the 5th graders who will be moving to middle school.

In a circle we shared autographs and debriefed our favorite times, activities, and laughed with talk of our busy year in second grade. Report cards had been passed and backpacks retrieved.

Excitement is growing as my student helpers and I are starting to shake the cans of shaving cream. Backpacks are placed safely in the hallway and we checked the clock, 25 minutes for the magic of shaving cream to clean all the tables. There is nothing like the overpowering clean smell of shaving creamed tables.

The tables are ready and the first "shot" of cream is on the first table to begin our last activity. There is a commotion at the door.

In walks our very caring Room Mom and her youngest. The little sibling is carrying a clear plastic tub and inside is a small chick chirping his annoyance. The children looked with excitement and some of the children start moving toward the visitors.

Still armed with two cans of shaving cream and quickly collecting the others, I head toward the visitors. Sure enough there is a lone chick looking at me with weary eyes.

The students head to the circle quickly and tighten up the circumference at my direction. The Mom (referred to now as Chick Mom) picked up the chick and plopped it on our class rug inside the human fence. I'm having visions of chicken poop all over the rug. The students are talking and reaching excitedly- some grabbing. The baby chick is staggering across the rug, avoiding the many reaching fingers. The circle is growing even tighter and louder at this point.

With a traditional clap pattern, I'm able to regain some order, reminding the students that calm and quiet voices will help the chick.

My mind is still running the what-could-happen-scenario. I look up as the hospitality student tells me there is a visitor at the door. I break the circle as the assistant superintendent comes in. With a quick glance around the room he waves and makes a hasty retreat. As he is trying to get out the door, in walk two more Moms.

I notice the child who owns the chick has it in her hands. I'm not seeing anything on the floor yet!

I see the chick is not cute and fluffy as I expected but molting!

Chick Mom is keeping a good eye on the children and the chick as the two Moms try to approach me on the opposite side of the circle. The owner of the chick is saying, "Now everyone needs to hold Chickie."

No time to react as the two moms walk through the circle to present me with a gift from the students. Before I can respond the class broadcaster is saying it's almost the end of the day. The chick is flapping and trying to escape; oh, and coming from the intercom is the traditional, "goodbye, have a great summer, time for dismissal," from the principal.

Chick Mom makes a great catch as 27 second graders rise, and I am saying, "Be sure to wash your hands". The students are trying to find a position in line, preschooler bursts into tears, Gift Moms grab their students, looking rather surprised at the confusion.

In true teacher style, I gather my students, quiet them down and walk them to the front hallway to say good bye for the last time this school year.

Returning to the room I tactfully hustle the adults and their children out of the room.

Ah, no chicken poop! A successful visit. Through the door poured the first and second grade teams.

Have you ever thought about what teachers do with cans of shaving cream on the last day of school?

What an exit!

My Last Day

I am so excited. Today is my last day of school. I'm almost a third grader. Who will I have? I'll wear my tappy shoes, blue twirly skirt, and my favorite white top.

"Hey, Mom, Chickie is three weeks old. I've been sharing about him at Circle Time. Yes, Mrs. N knows all about Chickie. I told her about candling the eggs, and when we all woke up because he was coming out of the egg ...

"Maggie, put him down!... MOM! Maggie is holding Chickie by the neck!"

I know, I'll take Chickie to school. Mrs. N is going to think this is so great.

"I'm taking him to school. Mrs. N will just love seeing him...

"Why?...

"The bus driver won't care...

"Please, it's the last day! P L E E Z E, P LEEZE PLEEZE PLEEZE. Will you bring him

P L E E Z E?"

"Hi Ruth, guess what? My mom is going to bring my chick to school. He's three weeks old. My sister chases him around the house. Aren't these pancakes great? Will I see you ever again? Fifth graders are lucky; they are done with school. Oh, you go somewhere else next year?...

"That's right. I'll see you at the pool..."

"Bye – Oh, here's the card I made you."

Oh, it is almost 11 o'clock and Mom hasn't come yet. She promised. Where's Mom? Where's Chickie? Mrs. N has the shaving cream cans. Oh I just love doing this.

"Can we draw in the shaving cream, Mrs. N.? Do our table first...

"MOM! Everybody, Mom's here with Chickie!"

Wuhu, she made it.

"Everybody, here's Chickie. We just love him. Maggie is always chasing him so he is used to us...

"OK, everyone hold him. Come on Jimmy. He won't bite...

"Maggie, leave Chickie in the box...

"MOM, Maggie has Chickie by the neck! What are you doing?...

"Paper towels are over there...

"Mrs. N, didn't you love my surprise?... I knew everyone would want to see Chickie. Thanks for a fun year. I'll come back in the fall to visit and I'll bring Chickie back!"

What a great last day. I surprised Mrs. N. I'm gonna be a third grader. I'm gonna be a third grader!

CHAPTER 10

KATHLEEN REDDY-BUTKOVICH

Notebook Noticings

Worried we had lost the capacity to listen
She assigns herself a small non-speaking part.
Poised in the vestibule, an intersection
Between anonymity and declaration,
She waits.

Enter two talkers
Telling of today with yesterday's news.
Too busy to describe a life unlived,
Like sprinklers in the rain,
It's blah, blah, blah.

Exit two talkers
Reiterating, refuting, regurgitating.
Too certain to converse,
Like a metronome enforcing the score,
It's blah, blah.

Others come and go
With heavy lids, tight lips, sore feet.
Too tired to talk,

Like patients denying diagnosis,
It's blah.

Could so many have come
To the moment in life
When there were no words?
She leaves to wonder and to write.
Ah!

January Falls

Upper Tahquamenon is stock-still on bumpy, golden ice.
Surprises of noonday sun mesmerize all onlookers—
Pine marten and moose stand in the bounce of blaring light.
Blink. A winter dream comes to life.
Enchanted characters emerge from the frozen waterfall:
Zhivago and Lara embrace in Varykino,
Narnia's white witch schemes to annihilate believers,
Sir Shackleton endures an Antarctica adventure.
In the distance there is a faint splash;
Like the icicles, we will weep with the thaw.

L Street

Finally the hypotenuse
she leaves the triangle.
An instigating line—
moving through chaos unnoticed.
Stretched thin,
no longer
cornered
or playing the right angle,
she arrives
at the Greek Ball,
and enters with Odysseus.

Apology

The language of apology:
a silent shiver of regret,
the lull,
then the free-fall
of words
recounting
archival
transcripts.
Words
uttered, this time
with white gloved attention.
Holding each to the light—
a careful recant.

CHAPTER 11

NATASHA GAVROSKI

Where I'm from

I am from apple orchards and river snakes.

From split pea soup and Golden Corral birthdays—

(ninja turtle themed with just enough pink to make it 'girly').

I am from Lake Placid.

In the Adirondacks of picturesque upstate New York,

where our cabin waited patiently every summer.

I'm from fresh, homemade Burek in an old haunted house, (or so legend says…).

From a town where school was shut down for a week and a half,

Due to a blizzard.

I'm from RR #9 Willobob Terrace and fishing on Oswego Lake,

During a strong thunderstorm.

From broken collarbones to mom's cancer diagnosis.

I am from all of this.

An old wooden shelf—built during the birth of my house.

Carved with a letter opener I marked my mantra, my blessing of hope:

"Mechka ima stra, a ja nemam stra."**

I am from these strong words and sad times. These times filled with time, recorded by photos

And many memories never to be forgotten.

**An old Macedonian saying my grandmother would often live by, meaning, "the big grizzly bear might be afraid, but I'm not afraid!"

Seven Words

Oh that finicky woman with her nose up and pinky out. She adamantly refuses to indulge in my delectable, mouth-watering flavors. Sure, I have tried to bamboozle her a time or two, smothering myself in various dressings including cheeses such as cheddar and even Velveeta! Oh, how I have prayed for tyrotoxism to come over her; maybe then she will finally appreciate me. Her husband is a little better; at least he will pick at me and then when done will offer me to the canine next door, so I'm not entirely wasted. Oh woe is me. It's not easy being a green vegetable.

(Tyrotoxism, finicky, smother, delectable, bamboozle, mouth-watering, canine)

Untitled

The windows creaked as the wind blew against them, making a striking noise as if they were coming alive. Once what was a happy house, filled with laughter and children playing, was now a dreaded, cold and dark house.

The police did their investigation and concluded that "48 year old Martin Berdinand of Westbrook, Maryland did not know what to do with his chaotic and confused life, and in turn he took it out on his family by brutally slaughtering his two kids and wife and then hung himself." The reporters replied.

But no one knew how to explain this horror to the city or what to make of it. Westbrook had always been a quiet, small town and this inevitably changed the outlook of the entire area. No one wanted to live in Westbrook after such a horrible crime was committed. No one felt safe.

From the outside, the Berdinand family seemed to be a normal family. Despite the typical quarrels between Mr. And Mrs. Berdinand, the family usually resolved all arguments and problems without a problem. Martin was an electrician, and as a hobby he performed at the nearby Dante Theatre as a magician. He loved his career as an electrician but magic was his love.

His wife, Marianne hated the fact that he even bothered with magic. She believed it was an act of Satanism.

"Get that evil out of my house, Martin! I will not have the children exposed to that un God-like influence." She would often say to him. He would seldom talk back or argue with her. Instead, he would go upstairs with a blank look on his face in a zombie like state of being.

Upon finding the bodies two days after the crime, the police conducted an extensive investigation. Every room was thoroughly examined. In the family room lay Marianne Berdinand fully exposed with her hands and legs tied together, her back staked up on the fireplace with a sharp metal shaving. She was so tightly held in place like a thumbtack pressed in a corkscrew. It took two men to pull her down.

Upstairs in the kids' room they found Jenny and Matthew tied together with a rubber hose around their waist. Their hands chopped off with a kitchen butcher knife and placed in a basket beside them. Marianne had made that basket for them that past summer. The knife he used, still covered in dry blood, was placed beside the bed, leaving a trail of sprinkled blood on the cream, shag rug. The investigators were in shock and could only imagine what this gruesome act meant. The kids were shot twice in the back of the head.

In the master bedroom bathroom they found the body of Martin Berdinand. He had hung himself with a teal colored jump rope.

"Well I'll be damned; the monster took the easy way out and killed himself." Officer Malone said, crossing his arms as he gazed at the body as if it were an art exhibit.

The paramedic on the scene walked over to Martin to take his pulse.

Holding his cold, stiff neck, "Yeah, he is confirmed dead. You might want to call the station and tell them we will need more for cleanup."

"Come on boys, let's get some something to cut this rope and get this animal down." Officer Malone replied.

The investigators stepped outside for a minute to take a breath away from the stale air in the house.

"Of all my years on the force, I have never seen such a grotesque sight," said one officer, brushing the sweat off his forehead with the back of his palm.

"My kids used to see him at the Dante every fall," said another officer.

As they returned to the scene of Martin's body, to their amazement nothing was there but the jump rope cut in two. The body of Martin was nowhere to be found.

The investigators quickly covered the scene. It was determined that Martin had killed his own family and then killed himself. A meeting was held the same night with Mayor Rudy and the police force.

"We cannot allow this crime to devastate our town. We have a reputation to upkeep," said Mayor Rudy, pounding his fist on the wooden desk. "The moment the townspeople get wind of this, chaos will follow."

"Mayor, the people already know something has happened. Investigators have been flooding the scene all day. The neighbors watched as the bodies were taken out of the house," Officer Malone replied.

"You must not tell them the truth. Tell them the case is closed and Martin was found dead. His actions were due to a mental breakdown and nothing is to be feared."

The truth is the police never found Martin. The investigators closed the case just as quickly as they opened it. Even to this day only one person knows the true whereabouts of Martin. Perhaps he is a Bob in your local town renting a small apartment with poor furnishings, or maybe he is in his room thinking and regretting his mishaps of the past. Perhaps this was Martin's Grand Finale, *my* final performance.

Written after a visit of the grounds at Meadow Brook Hall in Rochester, Michigan

Tears:
Ageless spots documenting time,
Dark nights with darker days are
Masked by champagne glasses and caviar.
Blood:
Creeping in the spines of
Flattened bricks on the ground,
Dried up and silenced.
Lies:
Cocktail hours and evening satchel drinks,
Between ink and pen, all faith is lost
In the name of a dollar.

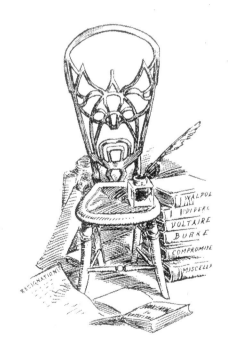

CHAPTER 12

ELIZABETH DAVIS

Lover of Rainbows: A Personal Narrative

Sitting in the woods near the Meadow Brook mansion, I hear the wind blowing through the trees like a gentle whisper. As I look up, the leaves flutter like a lace curtain blowing in the breeze from an open window. In this place I think of the poets I love – especially Wordsworth, lover of rainbows. I remember a poem he wrote about always wanting to be a lover of nature for as long as he lived. Hearing the birds chattering above, I am also reminded of that line from <u>Hamlet</u> where Hamlet is ready to face a certain death and says, "There is more providence in the fall of a sparrow…we defy augery…the readiness is all." I long to live a fearless life, free from the anxieties and pressures of family, finances, and career. I wish I could free my mind like that, to be a Wordsworth, a Romantic, a lover of rainbows and Tintern Abbeys, or to be a Hamlet, finally ready to face problems after all of the running, and to be able to sit in the woods and just relax.

I had a Wordsworth moment with my four-year-old son, Owen, a few weeks ago. At twilight we took a walk to the edge of the woods. All was quiet. Owen's hand wrapped around my pointer finger. We saw two deer emerge at the edge of the woods. They peered at us quizzically. Owen and I peered back. It was one of the only times I've observed Owen hushed in amazement. We stood there, the pair of us observing them…mirror objects of interest. Suddenly, the magical moment was over, and the deer ran back into the woods, the crash of broken leaves ruining the moment that seemed to last forever, but was in probably only a few seconds.

Still hand in hand, Owen bent his little blond head and crouched to the ground. He felt the outline of a deer track pressed into the hardened dirt. We followed the tracks as far as we could then walked back home in hushed silence, all the while his little hand wrapped in mine, his eyes wide in wonder.

I hope that my son will carry this memory with him as I carry it with me. When he is older and walks through the woods, will a crackle of branches remind him of the moment we shared? Will the touch of a gentle breeze awaken the memory of his hand holding mine? Will he remember his mother's love that pours from my heart like a rainbow spilling to earth? "My heart leaps up when I behold a rainbow in the sky." My heart will forever leap up when I remember this moment, and through difficult times, the memory sustains me.

Thoughtful Alphabets

The Storm
Anticipating blitzkrieg,
Clouds darken.
Electricity flashing,
Gusty heavens,
Intensifying joules,
Kinetic lightning:
Magnificent.
Noisy outbursts
Pouring quickly.
Rains streaming,
Thunder unleashed,
Violent water.
Exploding yellow zigzags.

The Great Diaper Disaster

Jeff was thirteen and thought he knew everything. It was a sweltering July; the humidity hung in the air like a wet blanket. Sitting on the front porch, Jeff could hear his mom bustling about in the house. Everything had to be picked up and spotless before embarking on the annual Davis trip to Saskatchewan.

Bursting out of the house, Jeff's dad barked at him: "Get your brother and get in the car. It's time to go." Jeff unpeeled the shorts sticking to his legs and went searching for Chris. He found him attempting to catch frogs from the ditch near the dirt road where they lived.

"Time to go."

Chris rolled his eyes. Jeff knew that for his brother Chris, catching frogs was much more enticing than an endless three-day road trip through the northern plains, despite the bags filled with crayons, blank paper, and homemade games their mother had so lovingly prepared. Chris dragged himself out of the ditch, looking down at his muddy shorts. Jeff and he shared a look. Mom would be mad. Maybe they could sneak into the car without her noticing. They shuffled up the gravel driveway towards the car. The family had borrowed a Ford station wagon from their friends since their own car could not be trusted to make it such a distance. Jeff and Chris were looking forward to sprawling in the long cabin in the back, marking their territory with Hardy Boy books and Kirk Gibson baseball cards.

Dad was already in the driver's seat, impatiently tapping on the steering wheel. His green fisherman's hat was propped on his head and his moustache looked droopy because of the heat. "C'mon, c'mon," he muttered to himself, "Your mother…"

They always left later than they planned.

Jeff's mother finally appeared at the front door, purse over one shoulder and diaper bag over the other. With a sigh and the baby Josh on her good hip, she hoisted herself into the station wagon. As the car pulled from the driveway, Josh began wailing. The trip had begun.

"Terry, did you remember the diapers?" Jeff's mom asked while eliciting a burp from Baby Josh.

"They are strapped to the top of the car. I used the bungee cords from the garage."

When they made these long trips to Grenfell, Saskatchewan, they would stay po0for about a month. With the additional baby gear, the station wagon was packed to capacity.

Dad turned on the air conditioning, and a cool breeze blew over him and into the backseat. Jeff was thankful they had borrowed this car and had the luxury of the air so that he did not have to sweat his way to the Great Plains of Canada. Josh had settled down by now and nestled into his mother's neck.

The station wagon bumped along the dirty gravel of 24 Mile Rd. Jeff pulled out *The Swiss Family Robinson* from his bag and began reading. As he got to the part where the family's boat was shipwrecked on the island, the family swerved onto the ramp to I-75. The station wagon lurched a bit as Dad pushed on the accelerator to match the speed of the other highway traffic, but it eventually coaxed itself to steady speed.

Jeff's father was a fearless driver. He had grown up in the hills of Pittsburgh and when vacationing there over Christmas, Jeff remembered being terrified of the way his dad had launched over the snow and ice, practically sliding down the deep embankments on the road of snow.

All of a sudden, Jeff heard a thud …and then another. Startled, he looked out the backseat window. White clouds were bursting behind them, thumping on the trunk of the station wagon, then launching on the highway. Jeff and Chris gazed out the back window fascinated, unable to look away from the scene unfolding before them. The diapers were breaking from their bungee cord prison and were firing on the traffic behind them, like boulders being hurled from an ancient catapult. As Jeff looked out the back window, he saw the face of the man in the car behind them change dramatically from a sleepy daze to a look of horror, as three large, plastic bags full of diapers flew off of the top of their station wagon and exploded all over his front windshield.

"Terry!" Mother screamed as she realized what was happening. Another diaper hit the hood and bounced off. Horns began to honk in protest of this onslaught.

Dad swerved and parked on the shoulder. It looked as if it had snowed in the middle of July. As cars zoomed by, the family would get bizarre looks from the passengers. It sounded like gunshots were going off all over the place as the diapers exploded when people ran over them.

"Stay in the car," Dad commanded the family.

Looking up and down I-75, Jeff's dad bobbed and weaved between the cars and semi-trucks. Jeff could see his white head bending over, grabbing a diaper and sprinting to the shoulder. Dad had better than 20/20 vision. He could spot a mole burrowing tunnels in the yard from across the street. With such acuity of vision, Dad spotted the diapers on the highway and scooped them up without being run over by a semi-truck.

The family sat in the car in silence. Jeff was wide-eyed, staring out the window. He was also worried. Were diapers worth his father's life? His mother was biting her lower lip while her eyes were blazing with fear and anger. Baby Josh, oblivious to the catastrophe, was dropping a rattle to the floor which Mom kept picking up and returning absentmindedly.

After what seemed like hours but was in actuality only a few minutes, Dad returned to the car, bearing the diapers he had been able to salvage.

"This is all I could get. I'm sorry, Connie."

"Terry, those diapers are not worth getting yourself killed!"

In a move that stunned the entire family, Dad piled the diapers back onto the the roof of the car. He flung the bungee cords over the stacks of diapers and pulled them tight. This led to a big argument about why someone would be so dumb as to make the same mistake twice.

"They're not going anywhere now," he muttered.

"Terry, what in the world are you doing?" Mom asked incredulously.

Jeff stared at his father. Maybe he was truly insane.

Dad did not respond but hopped back into the driver's seat. Everyone was quiet. Chris began sorting his baseball cards. Mom's faced was flushed. Jeff rolled his eyes. Dad started the car and turned on the radio. NewsRadio 950 a.m. came on.

"Traffic and weather on the eights," the announcer said. "We have a report of diapers in the road on I-75 just north of M-59. Drivers should use caution when approaching this area."

Dad changed the radio to Kenny Rogers and began humming along. Jeff settled back into his seat and picked up his book. He sighed as he remembered the phrase he had learned in school: "Those who do not learn from the past are doomed to repeat it." This incident eventually became known in the Davis family as the "Great Diaper Disaster" and was revisited and retold at Christmas, Easter, and any other occasion revolving around food and reminiscing. But for Jeff at this time, it reiterated what he had known all along: It was going to be a long trip.

My Favorite Day of the Week

The light starts to stream in the window. I take a couple extra sucks from my pacifier and slowly stretch my tiny arms. I lift my head covered in fine blond hair from the pile of blankets I like to heap under me so I feel like I am sleeping on a mountain of soft wool. I untangle my fingers from the holes on my favorite white blanket that I grab and curl around me as I sleep. I slowly get up to my knees and listen…there is no sound from anywhere in the house. Thinking I'd like to have some fun, I take all my pillows and blankets and promptly throw them over the side of my crib; I laugh – such a fun game! But, now I have nothing to play with! I climb and look over the side of the crib at the pile of bedding, Elmos, and stuffed bears now amassed on the floor. I tromp around on my mattress then I bang the dresser next to my bed. The hard wood against my fist hurts a bit, but the loud noise echoes wonderfully. I fling my pacifier across the room, open my mouth and start yelling, "Mommy!!!" I look toward the door…no Mommy. Apparently, my yell was not loud enough. I keep screaming Mommy until eventually it turns into a whine. Finally, after an eternity of waiting, my mother stumbles in. She looks at me through heavy eyelids and mumbles, "Why are you up so early?" I giggle and fling myself back onto the bed. I like to play a game of bouncing away when she tries to lift me up from my bed. Eventually, Mommy picks me up and kisses the top of my head. I wrap my arms around her neck and give her a big Jacob hug. The day has begun.

Our Writing Community

We are 12 professionals who came together for four weeks.

We are a community of trust built in that short time.

We are educators of the very young and more mature.

We are words and phrases: preface, France, protocol, *Moby Dick*, *Ish*, darkness, mysterious, laughter, flip flops, xenophile, butterfly sigh, hardboiled eggs, families, bikinis, Snickers, baking soda, craft.

We are cheese, crackers, fruit, vegetables,
Tootsie Pops, and Lazybones.

We are sharing, caring, trusting, supportive, diverse, and non-judging.

We are Meadow Brook Writing Project 2010 and so much more.

by Carolyn Newell